WITHDRAWN

Turkey at the Crossroads
From Crisis Resolution to EU Accession

Prepared by a team led by Reza Moghadam

INTERNATIONAL MONETARY FUND
Washington DC
2005

© 2005 International Monetary Fund

Production: IMF Multimedia Services Division

Cataloging-in-Publication Data

Turkey at the crossroads : from crisis resolution to EU accession / prepared by a team led
  by Reza Moghadam—Washington, D.C. : International Monetary Fund, 2005
        p.   cm.—(Occasional paper) ; 242

    Includes bibliographical references
    ISBN 1-58906-386-4

  1. Turkey—Economic conditions. 2. Turkey—Economic conditions—Statistics.
3. Inflation (Finance)—Turkey. 4. Debts, Public—Turkey. 5. Labor market—Turkey.
I. Moghadam, Reza. II. Occasional paper (International Monetary Fund ; no. 242
HC492.T87 2005

Price: US$25
(US$22 to full-time faculty members
and students at universities and colleges)

Please send orders to:
International Monetary Fund, Publication Services
700 19th Street, N.W., Washington, D.C. 20431, U.S.A.
Tel.: (202) 623-7430   Telefax: (202) 623-7201
E-mail: publications@imf.org
Internet: http://www.imf.org

recycled paper

Contents

Figures

CONTENTS

Preface

This Occasional Paper analyzes the transformation of Turkey's economic performance under its reform program supported by the International Monetary Fund, and sets out guideposts for the reform agenda that lies ahead. The paper was prepared by a team led by Reza Moghadam. The authors—Oya Celasun, Xavier Debrun, Mark Griffiths, Mats Josefsson, Christian Keller, Christoph Klingen, Chris Lane, Cheng Hoon Lim, David Marston, Donal McGettigan, Ashoka Mody, Ernesto Ramirez Rigo, Martin Schindler, and Mathew Verghis—include staff who have worked closely on the IMF program in Turkey, together with members of a number of the IMF's functional departments, in particular the Research Department, as well as World Bank staff.

The analysis is based on data available as of July 2004. However, more recent data do not alter the thrust of the analysis.

The authors would like to thank Michael Deppler, Susan Schadler, and Odd Per Brekk for their guidance and advice on these studies, and also for deepening our understanding of the economic issues facing Turkey more generally. We are also grateful to the Turkish authorities and to participants in seminars held in Ankara and Istanbul for discussions and comments, which have improved the papers. Chanpheng Dara provided excellent research assistance throughout, while Julie Burton, Connie Strayer, and Alimata Kini Kabore ably assisted in preparing the manuscript. The External Relations Department edited the manuscript and coordinated production of the publication.

The opinions expressed in this paper are solely those of its authors and do not necessarily reflect the views of the International Monetary Fund, its Executive Directors, or the Turkish authorities.

I Overview

Mark Griffiths and Reza Moghadam

Almost five years after the 2000–01 economic crisis, the fortunes of the Turkish economy have been transformed. The economy has grown rapidly for three successive years, inflation has fallen from 70 percent at the end of 2001 to single digits, both nominal and real interest rates have dropped sharply, and the government debt ratio has fallen significantly, improving prospects for debt sustainability. Maintaining and advancing these gains will be the key policy challenge in the coming years. Against this backdrop, this Occasional Paper reviews policy performance in the key areas of growth, inflation, debt, fiscal and financial sector reform, and labor markets. The analysis aims both to assess the effectiveness of reforms pursued since the crisis and to provide guideposts for the future direction of economic policy.

Improving Turkey's growth performance has been a key objective of the 2001–04 reform program, through both macroeconomic stabilization and structural economic reform. For Turkey, higher growth can contribute significantly to debt sustainability, raising living standards toward European Union (EU) levels, and reducing unemployment. Chapter II documents Turkey's growth record and the factors that explain it. Performance has been slightly better than the world average, especially since 1980, mainly because of increased openness to trade, financial market liberalization, and broader economic reform efforts. But Turkey could have done much better than it did. One key factor holding back the country's growth and increasing its volatility has been the lack of discipline in fiscal, monetary, and financial policies. This has destabilized the economy and reduced its trend growth rate. Looking ahead, the analysis suggests that Turkey has the potential to grow at a rate similar to those of the East Asian economies. Indeed, the recent decline in inflation should help boost the growth rate in the future. However, maintaining policy discipline and ongoing structural reforms will be essential to sustain high growth and reduce volatility.

Reducing high and persistent inflation has been another focus of reform policies aimed at enhancing Turkey's medium-term economic performance. Inflation first took off in the 1970s, peaking at more than 100 percent with the second oil price shock, and then rising again in the mid-1990s. The uniqueness of this experience lies not so much in the high level of inflation itself but in the fact that Turkey managed to live with these high rates for so long, rather than exploding into hyperinflation or launching a successful disinflation effort. With such high inflation over such a long period of time, there was a concern that price-setting had become more backward-looking, which would have complicated the task of reducing inflation. Instead, Chapter III finds that much of this persistent inflation was self-fulfilling: the inflation process was driven more by expectations of future high inflation than by formal backwards indexation. Fiscal policy turns out to be a key determinant of these expectations, so the reform program's focus on generating sustained, high primary surpluses has been central to the success of disinflation.

Balance sheet weaknesses in the financial and corporate sectors have contributed to Turkey's propensity to fall into crisis. Chapter IV documents these preexisting weaknesses and shows how they were magnified by the depreciation of the Turkish lira in 2001 and the increase in interest rates during the crisis. The chapter also shows how private sector balance sheets have since been restored, in part because of the economic recovery and success in macroeconomic stabilization, but also because some of the vulnerabilities have been transferred to the government, which has taken on greater foreign currency and interest rate risk. Although balance sheets have improved considerably and risks have fallen, the analysis shows that Turkey still remains vulnerable, especially while dollarization remains so extensive. This again points to the need for continued low inflation, which should encourage the demand for lira-denominated assets, and reduce vulnerabilities.

The weakness of the government's balance sheet has also been a source of instability for Turkey's economy. For this reason, the reform program has stressed efforts to ensure the sustainability of the debt and improve its structure. Chapter V surveys the literature on the appropriate level of public debt for emerging market economies such as Turkey, and concludes that projecting debt sustainability is not enough. Turkey's external debt ratio is well above levels considered safe for emerging markets, while its high level of public debt raises concerns about fiscal dominance, which could undermine the effectiveness of monetary policy in reducing inflation. These considerations suggest the importance of targeting a significant reduction in government debt. But achieving such a reduction will take many years. In the meantime, effective management of this debt is essential to ensure that it is safely rolled over and that its structure is made more resilient to shocks. Chapter VI reviews the authorities' debt management strategy, and gauges their success in issuing securities that more closely match investor needs, widening the investor base, deepening the liquidity of benchmark bonds, and improving the Treasury's risk management.

Improving the government balance sheet depends on reducing Turkey's government debt, and fiscal adjustment and sustained primary surpluses are essential to accomplish this. Chapter VII estimates the factors that determine primary surpluses across countries, and finds that Turkey's fiscal adjustment since 2000 has been impressive, and marks a significant break with past performance. However, the risk is that this break cannot be sustained, and that Turkey's primary surplus will revert to the lower levels predicted by the cross-country analysis. To prevent this, structural fiscal reforms will be needed to sustain this adjustment.

Chapter VIII complements this analysis by looking at Turkey's history of fiscal adjustment in more detail. It finds that the adjustment since 2000 has relied mainly on tax increases. Spending on investment has been cut, but this has been offset by increased current expenditure. Based on the experience of other countries, such an adjustment could prove difficult to sustain. The emergence of a stronger and more disciplined government, together with efforts to curtail quasi-fiscal operations in state enterprises and spending by extra-budgetary funds, should help. But a redirection of the adjustment toward cuts in current spending, and less reliance on temporary tax increases, would help make the current fiscal adjustment easier to sustain.

Reform of the financial sector has also been at the heart of the program. Such reform has been essential both to prevent any recurrence of the weaknesses that precipitated the 2000–01 crisis and added to the government's debt burden, and also to foster increased lending and recovery in the real sector. After describing the outbreak of the banking crisis and the measures the authorities took to contain it, Chapter IX explains the reforms that have been introduced, including the restructuring of state banks and the recapitalization of private banks. This strategy has largely succeeded in strengthening the banking system and maintaining the confidence of depositors. Even so, both asset recovery and the resolution of intervened banks have been slow, and this has increased the costs of the crisis. Further reforms are needed to enhance the effectiveness of banking supervision and asset resolution.

Chapter X considers recent developments in the labor market, particularly Turkey's low employment rate, the increase in unemployment, and low labor force participation rates, especially for women. Increases in labor productivity have helped Turkey maintain its competitiveness and reduced pressures on inflation, but at the cost of weak employment growth. One obstacle to employment growth is the cost of complying with recent legislation on statutory employment protection. The cost of such compliance is more than twice the average of the nations of the Organization for Economic Cooperation and Development (OECD). These new regulations have helped entrench the existing dual labor market structure, making it harder for new entrants to the labor force to find work in the well-paid formal sector. Labor market reform may be needed to ensure that recent improved growth performance translates into reduced unemployment.

II Economic Growth in Turkey, 1960–2000

Ashoka Mody and Martin Schindler

In the face of a global economic slowdown after 1980, countries that maintained or increased growth rates typically expanded trade and deepened their financial systems as well. Growth was set back when countries were unable to resolve multiple claims on fiscal resources and experienced high fiscal volatility, inflation, and rising levels of debt. Where all these factors were favorable, as in East Asia, growth was exceptionally rapid. Turkey benefited from the entrepreneurship made possible through trade and financial sector liberalization in 1980, but fiscal policy instability and inflation constrained its growth. Looking ahead, as the growth potential of Turkey's trade reforms begins to reach its maximum levels, the nation will need continued structural reforms to spur increased entrepreneurship in a competitive environment, while maintaining a commitment to fiscal policy discipline.

Turkey's per capita income grew between 1960 and 1980 at about 2.3 percent per year. Although world growth slowed after 1980 from 2.5 to 1 percent annually, Turkey continued to grow at an annual rate of 2.3 percent, thereby improving its performance relative to the world average. An important turning point in Turkish economic history occurred in 1980, as noted by Krueger (2004, p. 2):

> The ambitious program that began on January 26, 1980 was intended to mark the start of serious economic reform efforts after years of false starts. A big shake-up in both policymaking and policy signaled a completely fresh approach. The reforms had three main aims: economic stabilization, including a reduction in the rate of inflation; a deliberate shift away from import substitution and towards an export-oriented economy; and a move towards a more market-oriented economy.

Early results from the reforms were favorable, but sources of policy instability and macro uncertainty, which had long been endemic, quickly reasserted themselves and rose to a new level of virulence. Thus, Turkey achieved solid growth but also suffered increasing volatility, giving up hard-won output gains in frequent and severe crises.

Growth was helped especially by trade and financial sector liberalization, which marked an important break with the past and allowed for the vibrant expression of Turkish entrepreneurship. Early introduction of export subsidies was followed by reduction of tariff and nontariff barriers, culminating in the customs union with the European Community in 1996. In the financial sector, deregulation of interest rates was followed by enhancement of accounting standards and the opening up of the capital account in 1989. Trade and credit expansion made possible by the liberalization have been Turkey's principal sources of growth since 1980, though the growth dividend hit diminishing returns in the 1990s. Turkey's increasing reliance on manufactured exports brought the added benefit of reducing exposure to external (terms of trade) volatility; in contrast, vulnerabilities in the financial sector have remained a source of concern.

The main source of instability, however, was the stop-go pattern of economic management, reflected in a high level of fiscal discretionary spending, high and rising inflation, and an increasing external debt position. Though inflation fell briefly in the early 1980s, it rose to new highs thereafter, as did volatility in fiscal expenditures. A sharp deterioration in the fiscal position in the 1990s and a continued rise in debt levels eventually ended in the economic crisis and contraction in 2001. In such an environment of uncertainty, domestic investment and productivity growth were held back.

This chapter places Turkey's growth experience in an international context, comparing the growth achievements of a cross-section of countries between 1980 and 2000 with their growth in the preceding two decades. The regression results do not prove causation but should be viewed as an attempt to approximately quantify the contribution to growth of the two opposing forces of liberalization and macro instability. The analysis suggests that the key challenge for Turkey is to continue to increase the scope for private entrepreneurship through structural reforms, while instituting fiscal discipline to reduce macro uncertainty and hence spur further increases in productivity and investment.

The chapter first highlights key features of Turkey's economic performance before examining the correlates of growth, placing Turkey in a comparative perspective.

The main quantitative results based on cross-country growth analyses are then presented, including the decomposition of growth into total factor productivity growth and investment growth. Finally, the chapter briefly examines the sources of macro instability and asks, in particular, whether economic liberalization generates domestic conflicts over limited resources that result in volatility, ultimately hurting growth.

Recent Growth and Volatility Trends

Over the past several decades, Turkey has struggled to raise—and then keep—its per capita income above the world average. Turkey came close to the global average as early as 1976 at the peak of a short-lived growth spurt, but the effort collapsed during the debt crisis of 1979–80 (Figure 2.1). Adopting a series of major reforms, the country then embarked on an apparently more sustained trend toward closing the gap with the global economy. In 1988, Turkey's level of per capita GNP surpassed the global average for the first time in the twentieth century, ultimately exceeding global average GNP by 10 percent in 2000. Unfortunately, this trend ended with yet another growth collapse in 2001, reducing output by about 9 percent and bringing per capita income back to almost precisely the global average.[1]

Turkey, therefore, can be characterized over the past quarter century or so as having had above-average growth performance but also a high degree of volatility. At about 2.3 percent per year, Turkey's per capita income grew somewhat faster than world per capita income between 1960 and 2000. Turkish performance far surpassed that of sub-Saharan Africa, where per capita incomes grew at less than 0.6 percent a year over the same period, but Turkey lagged behind East Asian economies, where annual per capita growth was more than one percentage point higher (Table 2.1).

Notably, Turkey grew at an average rate of 2.3 percent annually not only from 1960–2000, but also during each of the 20-year subperiods (1960–80 and 1981–2000). While Turkey's growth rate thus remained unchanged in absolute terms over the two subperiods, its relative growth performance actually improved, as world growth slowed in the second period (Figures 2.1 and 2.2). The 90 countries in the sample grew at an average rate of 2.6 percent annually over 1960–80 but at only 1.3 percent annually from 1981–2000. Because Turkish per capita output growth was relatively high after 1980, its per capita output exceeded the global average in 1988 (though that gain was subsequently lost in the 2001 crisis, which is not considered in the analysis below).

Though Turkey maintained respectably high growth rates, an important feature of the nation's growth from 1980 to 2000 was a sharp increase in volatility (Figure 2.3). An increase in volatility by itself is not a sign of concern—many East Asian countries have grown rapidly and experienced brief periods of high volatility. Indeed, Tornell, Westermann, and Martinez (2004) point out that the link between volatility and growth may be positive or negative. In this view, the deregulation of the financial sector is necessary to support higher growth, but financial sector fragilities may also lead to crises. The volatility may thus be a necessary price for achieving high long-term growth. Other research, such as that by Ramey and Ramey (1995), suggests that volatility may have no redeeming feature. An important question, therefore, is whether Turkey could have done better if volatility had been contained. As shown below, the increased volatility in Turkey was related to instability in fiscal and monetary policies that are associated with a growth-reducing effect.

Growth Accounting

A growth accounting exercise provides insights into the channels through which growth has occurred. Growth accounting decomposes observed output growth into components that can be attributed to the increased use of factor inputs and those due to growth in total factor productivity (TFP). As is conventional, we assume a constant returns-to-scale, Cobb-Douglas production function:

$$Y_t = A_t K_t^\alpha \left(h_t L_t \right)^{1-\alpha}$$

where Y is aggregate output, A is the level of technology, or TFP, K is the physical capital stock, h is the human capital stock per worker, L is the number of workers, and α is the elasticity of output with respect to physical capital. Expressing all variables in per-worker terms (denoted by small caps), taking log differences across time and omitting time indices, we obtain:

$$\Delta \log(y) = \Delta \log(A) + \alpha \Delta \log(k) + (1-\alpha) \Delta \log(h)$$

or

$$\Delta \log(A) = \Delta \log(y) - \alpha \Delta \log(k) - (1-\alpha) \Delta \log(h).$$

In Turkey and all comparator groups, the worldwide growth slowdown after 1980 was accompanied by a significant slowdown in TFP growth (Table 2.2),[2]

---

[1]Turkey's per capita GNP was $6,033 in 2001, measured in 1990 international Geary-Khamis dollars, compared with a world average of $6,049 (Maddison, 2001).

[2]The physical and human capital stock data underlying the growth accounting exercise are from Bosworth and Collins (2003). The GNP series is from Penn World Table Version 6.1 (Heston, Summers, and Aten, 2002).

Figure 2.1. Real Per Capita GDP
(In 1990 international Geary-Khamis dollars)

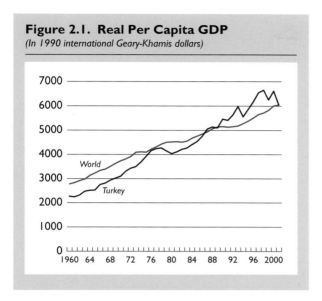

Figure 2.2. Real Per Capita GDP Growth
(Backward-looking 10-year average; in percent)

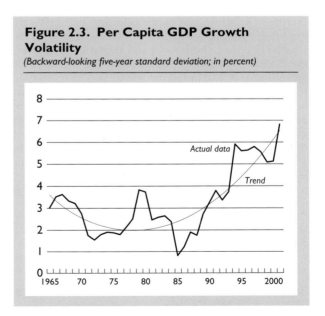

although Turkey's TFP decline was less pronounced. Physical capital growth, which decreased in all of the comparator groups, increased in Turkey, consistent with the observed increase in Turkish investment rates. Overall, then, Turkey's relative (and absolute) growth performance improved due to a more moderate slowdown in overall factor productivity, and to a rise in physical capital accumulation. Human capital appears to have grown in line with cross-country experience.

Table 2.1. Real Per Capita GDP Growth, 1960–2000
(Annual percent changes)

Developing countries	1.37
Latin America	1.37
Argentina	1.00
Brazil	2.77
Mexico	1.97
East Asia	3.45
South Asia	2.11
Middle East	2.74
Egypt	2.62
Greece	3.14
Israel	2.80
Turkey	2.33
Sub-Saharan Africa	0.57
Industrial countries	2.69
Germany	2.03
Japan	4.23
United States	2.49
All countries	1.80

Source: Penn World Table Version 6.1 (Heston, Summers, and Aten, 2002).

The remainder of this chapter considers the factors that were correlated with growth, then returns to the growth accounting exercise to examine whether these correlates worked through the productivity or investment channels.

Correlates of Growth

This section describes shifts in the overall macro and policy environment between the periods 1960–80 and 1980–2000, which are then the basis of a more formal cross-country regression analysis in the next section.

Figure 2.3. Per Capita GDP Growth Volatility
(Backward-looking five-year standard deviation; in percent)

Table 2.2. Growth Accounting, 1961–2000
(Annual percent changes)

	Per Capita GDP	TFP	Physical Capital	Human Capital
			1961–2000	
Turkey	2.33	0.92	1.01	0.40
Middle East	2.75	1.27	1.07	0.41
Upper-middle-income countries	2.45	0.97	1.08	0.40
All countries	1.98	0.73	0.91	0.34
			1961–1980	
Turkey	2.32	1.10	0.85	0.37
Middle East	3.71	1.94	1.38	0.39
Upper-middle-income countries	3.07	1.41	1.23	0.43
All countries	2.62	1.07	1.22	0.33
			1981–2000	
Turkey	2.35	0.73	1.19	0.43
Middle East	1.79	0.61	0.75	0.43
Upper-middle-income countries	1.83	0.53	0.94	0.36
All countries	1.33	0.37	0.62	0.34

Note: The table covers 73 countries from the sample for which Bosworth and Collins (2003) provide physical and human capital stock data. GDP data are from Penn World Table Version 6.1; total factor productivity (TFP) is calculated as the residual, as described in the text.

Of particular interest is the identification of variables that proxy policy changes that have sustained Turkey's growth and those that have been unfavorable to growth.[3]

Turkey experienced a substantial increase in the degree of trade openness and, consequently, in its trade-to-GNP ratio. Though the initial focus was on increased subsidies for exports, import barriers were gradually reduced starting in 1984, resulting in a substantial decline in both tariff and nontariff barriers by the mid-1990s (Krueger and Aktan, 1992; and Ozler and Yilmaz, 2004). In January 1996, Turkey reinforced its commitment to open trade by forming a customs union with the European Community (Erzan, Filiztekin, and Zenginobuz, 2003). Turkey adopted the European Union's common external tariff (about 4 percent for manufactured goods) against third country imports in 1996 and the preferential agreements the EU has concluded with third countries by 2001. At the same time, the EU, which had eliminated tariffs on most Turkish manufactures, committed to abolish quotas, particularly on textiles and clothing, and gradually on iron and steel (although use of antidumping legislation continues to be a source of nontariff barriers).

These measures resulted in a threefold increase in the trade ratio, from under 12 percent to about 38 percent between the first and second period considered in this chapter (Table 2.3). Figure 2.4 shows that the trade ratio had begun to level off following the initial round of reforms and was given a fillip in the lead up to and the period following entry into the EU customs union. Krueger (2004, p. 2) has concluded that ". . . the reforms introduced succeeded in shifting Turkey permanently towards a more export-oriented economy."

Most countries became more outward-oriented after 1980, as highlighted by the averages in Table 2.3. Turkey's experience was, therefore, consistent with a more generally observed increase in trade flows following liberalization of trade policy (Wacziarg and Welch, 2003). However, Turkey's performance was nevertheless remarkable, with the increase in its trade ratio representing the biggest relative increase in the sample.

In theory, more openness also makes a country more vulnerable to external shocks (Rodrik, 1999). However, Turkey's terms of trade volatility declined in the 1980s and 1990s—much of the export growth was

---

[3]All data are from the World Bank World Development Indicators database, except real GDP, which is from Penn World Table Version 6.1 (Heston, Summers, and Aten, 2002), schooling (from Barro-Lee, 2000), political constraints (from Fatás and Mihov, 2003), and the International Country Risk Guide measure (from Bosworth and Collins, 2003).

Table 2.3. Summary Statistics, Selected Variables

Variable	Region	1961–1980	1981–2000	1961–2000
Initial per capita GDP (U.S. dollars)	Turkey	2,833	4,520	2,833
	East Asia	4,076	8,474	4,076
	Latin America	3,626	4,996	3,626
	OECD	9,083	16,042	9,083
Average schooling (years)	Turkey	2.2	3.8	3.0
	East Asia	5.0	6.9	5.9
	Latin America	3.3	5.0	4.1
	OECD	7.1	8.7	7.9
Primary fiscal balance	Turkey	. . .	−4.7	−4.7
	East Asia	−2.9	0.0	−1.5
	Latin America	−2.7	−2.5	−2.6
	OECD	−3.6	−4.2	−3.9
Fiscal discretionary volatility	Turkey	5.3	9.6	7.5
	East Asia	4.5	3.8	4.1
	Latin America	10.0	9.0	9.5
	OECD	3.0	2.6	2.8
External volatility (standard deviation of terms of trade growth)	Turkey	10.3	4.5	7.4
	East Asia	10.2	6.9	8.6
	Latin America	12.7	11.3	12.0
	OECD	4.6	3.6	4.1
Inflation (percent)	Turkey	18.0	46.1	32.1
	East Asia	11.0	5.4	8.2
	Latin America	15.5	36.5	26.0
	OECD	7.7	5.2	6.5
External debt	Turkey	16.9	40.4	28.6
	East Asia	29.1	51.4	40.2
	Latin America	33.8	82.0	57.9
	OECD	. . .	. . .	. . .
Government size (government expenditure, % of GDP)	Turkey	10.3	10.7	10.5
	East Asia	13.1	13.3	13.2
	Latin America	10.8	12.2	11.5
	OECD	16.4	19.7	18.0
Trade openness (sum of exports & imports, % of GDP)	Turkey	11.4	37.7	24.6
	East Asia	80.9	111.6	96.3
	Latin America	46.0	53.9	49.9
	OECD	51.1	64.1	57.6
Investment (% of GDP)	Turkey	17.9	22.6	20.2
	East Asia	21.5	27.6	24.5
	Latin America	18.4	18.5	18.5
	OECD	23.3	20.5	21.9
Financial depth (growth in M2)	Turkey	2.9	7.5	5.2
	East Asia	6.2	6.2	6.2
	Latin America	4.6	2.8	3.7
	OECD	2.6	3.6	3.1
Financial depth (M2/GDP)	Turkey	18.8	24.3	21.5
	East Asia	33.5	60.8	47.2
	Latin America	19.1	29.1	24.1
	OECD	48.2	60.8	54.5
Political constraints	Turkey	0.41	0.51	0.46
	East Asia	0.40	0.57	0.49
	Latin America	0.24	0.44	0.34
	OECD	0.70	0.77	0.74

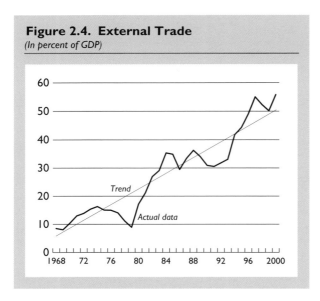

Figure 2.4. External Trade
(In percent of GDP)

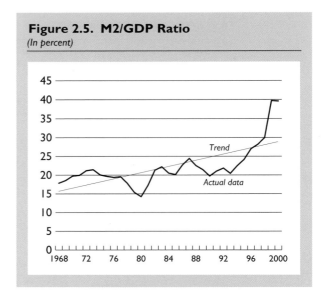

Figure 2.5. M2/GDP Ratio
(In percent)

from the manufacturing sector, which increased as a share of Turkish exports from about 36 percent in 1980 to over 90 percent in 2000—reducing the scope of macroeconomic instability that may stem from a volatile trading environment. Instead, investment as a share of GNP increased. Once again, the cross-country empirical evidence presented in Wacziarg and Welch (2003) shows that as countries have expanded trade flows, they also have stepped up their investment. Note, though, that despite these increases, investment shares in Turkey remained relatively low, especially compared with East Asian and Organization for Economic Cooperation and Development (OECD) economies, suggesting the scope for a further increase in investment rates.

As will be shown below, financial development also has had a generally positive influence on growth, spurred by liberalization initiated in 1980. In July of that year, ceilings were lifted on interest rates that banks paid and could charge. In 1985, protection of deposits through deposit insurance, standardization of accounting, and norms for the treatment of nonperforming loans were introduced (Sancak, 2002). The M2/GDP ratio, which had been flat to trending down in the 1970s, rose rapidly following the liberalization (Figure 2.5).[4]

---

[4]Despite its important contribution to growth, the financial sector still has significant weaknesses. The banking system is highly concentrated. In the past, weak banking practices, poor regulation, and lack of corporate governance made the banking system vulnerable. The operations of state banks posed particular difficulties. Macro and structural reforms are not unrelated. For example, Alper and Önis (2004) argue that endemic budget deficits, government ownership in the banking system, and failure to provide proper banking system regulation are intimately linked.

On the down side, macro instability increased, reflected in different forms. In general terms, the source of the instability was an untenable demand on fiscal resources. The most notable development after 1980 was a marked increase in fiscal discretionary volatility (Figure 2.6), a constructed measure reflecting unexpected changes in fiscal expenditure that are inconsistent with past policies or changes in the economic environment.[5] Specifically, using annual data over 1960–2000 for each country in the sample,[6] we estimate the equation:

$$\Delta G_{i,t} = \alpha_i + \beta_i \Delta Y_{i,t-1} + \gamma_i \Delta Y_{i,t-2} + \delta_i \Delta G_{i,t-1}$$
$$+ \eta_i' W_{i,t} + \varepsilon_{i,t}$$

where G is the logarithm of real government expenditures, Y is the logarithm of real GNP in constant local currency units, and W is a vector of controls, including terms of trade growth, inflation, inflation squared, and a time trend. The measure σ_i^f of fiscal volatility is defined as the standard deviation of the residual of the above regression equation. The intention is to abstract from fiscal responses to the economic cycle and other macroeconomic conditions, such as inflation and external developments. By also including lagged government expenditure growth, the measure of fiscal policy discretion can be interpreted as representing unexpected, cyclically adjusted deviations from a country's past fiscal policy stance that are unrelated to macroeconomic conditions.

---

[5]See Fatás and Mihov (2003) for a similar construction of a measure of discretionary fiscal volatility.

[6]The cross-country sample consists of 90 countries. However, because country coverage of many variables is not complete, sample sizes differ across regression specifications.

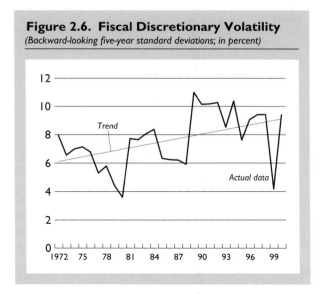

Figure 2.6. Fiscal Discretionary Volatility
(Backward-looking five-year standard deviations; in percent)

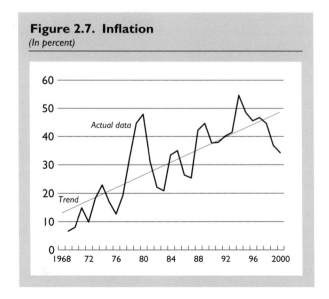

Figure 2.7. Inflation
(In percent)

Turkey's fiscal volatility increased notably at a time when such volatility was declining in other economically important regions. That this is not a purely statistical artifact is supported by analysis of the country's budgetary processes, which shows not only the inability to restrain aggregate deficits but also lack of transparency and the use of extrabudgetary devices to permit a high rate of discretionary expenditures (Celasun, 1990; and World Bank, 2001). Fiscal volatility has been shown to be a key contributor to overall growth volatility and might thus explain why Turkey's growth has become more volatile while growth has become more stable in most other countries (as noted above in the discussion of Figure 2.2). Moreover, several studies (Fatás and Mihov, 2003; and Mody and Schindler, 2004) have shown fiscal discretionary volatility to be "harmful" volatility, with a robust, negative effect on growth. That negative relationship is also confirmed in the econometric analyses presented below.

The period from 1981–2000 was characterized by a large average budget deficit and significantly higher inflation—over 46 percent annually. While moderate inflation is typically found to have no significant correlation with growth, high inflation tends to be associated with lower growth, and inflation in Turkey rose sharply over the past several decades (Figure 2.7). Lastly, Turkey's external debt increased rapidly, much more so than in the average country (Figure 2.8).[7]

Note that Turkey managed to maintain the size of government at a constant level, not only lower than the

sample average, but also avoiding the increased volume of government spending most other countries exhibited. Thus, it was not changes in the size of the government per se that were harmful for growth, but rather a decreased predictability of expenditure growth as well as the deficits that were reflected in inflation.

Cross-Country Regression Analysis

The reasons behind the change in Turkey's relative position between 1960–80 and 1981–2000 can be determined by regressing changes in average growth in the subperiods on changes in key policy variables.

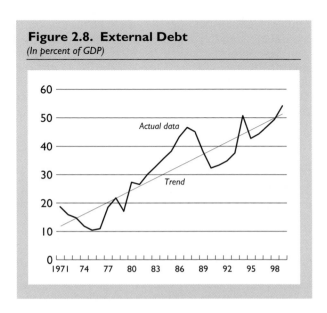

Figure 2.8. External Debt
(In percent of GDP)

---

[7]Several studies, most notably Pattillo, Poirson, and Ricci (2004), have found external debt levels to have a negative (if nonlinear) impact on growth. Because the available external debt data are fairly limited, however, they are not included in the regressions.

The main variables identified are fiscal volatility, inflation, and changes in trade openness. Convergence effects are controlled for by including the difference of the two subperiods' initial per capita GNP (that is, growth in the first subperiod).

First, however, an alternative growth explanation warrants mention. In an influential study, Rodrik (1999) argues that in recent decades, countries exposed to external volatility were especially likely to suffer from growth slowdowns—more so in divided societies, especially if they had weak internal institutions to manage the conflicts that arise in conditions of economic volatility. If this were the case, Turkey's drive to open its economy to more trade would have had a harmful effect. Although Turkey has a very high level of inequality, its external volatility was never high and, importantly, declined after 1980 as the country became an exporter of manufactured goods. To pursue these issues in more detail, a composite measure is constructed—referred to as "conflict" in analogy to Rodrik (1999)—as the product of external trade volatility times trade openness (1981–2000 averages) times the 1960–2000 average of income inequality times 100*(1-ICRG1982), divided by the composite measure's standard deviation.

Column (1) of Table 2.4 shows Rodrik's finding: the conflict variable is indeed negatively related to growth. However, a substantial and statistically significant fraction of Turkish growth remains unexplained (as indicated by the Turkish "dummy" variable). More importantly, by its construction, interacting four different variables, the conflict measure implicitly assumes that trade openness is harmful. When trade openness is entered by itself in column (2), it is positively related to growth and the conflict measure is insignificant. When the fiscal volatility measure is also included in column (3) and inflation in column (4), the conflict measure further loses statistical significance, with fiscal volatility, inflation, and trade openness all statistically relevant descriptors of growth and the Turkish dummy statistically insignificant.[8] The conclusion is that the conflict measure has little importance in the case of Turkey. In the following section, the specification in column (5) is thus taken out as the starting point for examining other potential growth correlates.

Key Growth Results

Table 2.5 presents the main results, especially in column (6). All key variables are highly significant, except

the dummy for Turkey, meaning that Turkey's change in growth is well explained. The partial scatter plots in Figure 2.9, based on the regression specification in column (6), confirm that the results are not being driven by a few outliers. The results lend support to the hypothesis that Turkey underwent conflicting changes in the period after 1980. The trade share increased dramatically and provided the main impetus to growth. At the same time, financial sector development also helped. These positive influences were weakened by deterioration in fiscal and monetary discipline, measured by greater fiscal volatility and high inflation.

These main results are robust to the inclusion of a number of other variables. In particular, an increase in external volatility did not lower growth. While an increase in the size of government was related to a decrease in growth, the effect was not significant.

From a technical point of view, the regressions are simple ordinary least squares (OLS) and as such present correlations, not causal relationships. However, given its construction, reverse causation is less likely in the case of the fiscal volatility measure, as Fatás and Mihov (2003) also argue. Also, while trade flows could have increased in response to an increase in growth, rather than the other way around, the results of Wacziarg and Welch (2003) suggest that trade flows are influenced by the policy of trade liberalization. For Turkey, the timing of the increase in trade flows coincides well with liberalization. Nevertheless, the results are interpreted here as merely approximations of the quantitative contributions to growth of the two opposing forces of liberalization and macro instability.

Decomposing Growth

Overall, at .0313 percentage point, there was essentially no change in Turkey's growth over the two subperiods. But referring to column (6) in Table 2.5, the change in Turkey's growth can be decomposed into its various sources[9] in order to examine how the various factors interacted in keeping aggregate growth unchanged. In order to do this, the regression in column (6) in Table 2.5 is repeated without the Turkey dummy and the resulting coefficients are applied to the actual variable outcomes for Turkey. The results are summarized in Table 2.6. Focusing on the four policy variables, the main growth-reducing factors were (i) the increase in fiscal volatility, associated with a growth reduction of .48 percentage points, and (ii) the rise in inflation, associated with reduced growth of .7 percentage point. The main growth-enhancing factors were (i) the sharp increase in external trade, associated

---

[8]The data also show that the correlation coefficient between "conflict" and "external shocks" is .9, suggesting that the conflict variable is mostly picking up external shocks (terms of trade volatility multiplied by the trade share), with little variation stemming from institutions and inequality or their interactions with external shocks.

---

[9]The unexplained part, represented by the Turkey dummy, is very small and insignificant and we therefore ignore it.

Table 2.4. Cross-Country Growth Difference Regressions
(Dependent variable is GDP growth difference)

	(1)	(2)	(3)	(4)	(5)
Conflict	−0.401	−0.291	−0.208	−0.112	
	(0.025)**	(0.134)	(0.274)	(0.530)	
Fiscal volatility			−1.009	−0.710	−0.959
			(0.015)**	(0.062)*	(0.006)***
Inflation				−0.045	−0.038
				(0.000)***	(0.000)***
Initial per capita GDP	−2.196	−2.304	−2.201	−2.652	−2.292
	(0.002)***	(0.001)***	(0.001)***	(0.000)***	(0.000)***
Trade openness		1.532	1.753	1.269	2.188
		(0.116)	(0.058)*	(0.151)	(0.004)***
Turkey dummy	1.209	−0.043	0.529	1.310	0.870
	(0.000)***	(0.961)	(0.553)	(0.121)	(0.256)
Observations	70	70	70	70	90
Adjusted R^2	0.143	0.171	0.244	0.374	0.311

Note: Numbers in parentheses are robust p-values. Significance levels are *10%; **5%; ***1%. All regressions include a constant. All variables except conflict are period differences. The conflict variable is constructed as in Rodrik (1999).

Table 2.5. Additional Cross-Country Growth Difference Regressions
(Dependent variable is GDP growth difference)

	(1)	(2)	(3)	(4)	(5)	(6)
Fiscal volatility	−0.959	−0.928	−0.956	−0.950	−0.911	−0.850
	(0.006)***	(0.015)**	(0.007)***	(0.008)***	(0.009)***	(0.022)**
Inflation	−0.038	−0.040	−0.038	−0.041	−0.038	−0.045
	(0.000)***	(0.000)***	(0.000)***	(0.001)***	(0.000)***	(0.000)***
Initial per capita GDP	−2.292	−2.506	−2.267	−2.432	−2.270	−2.500
	(0.000)***	(0.000)***	(0.000)***	(0.000)***	(0.000)***	(0.000)***
Trade openness	2.188	2.222	2.203	2.115	2.014	2.128
	(0.004)***	(0.006)***	(0.004)***	(0.005)***	(0.013)**	(0.003)***
Turkey dummy	0.870	1.071	0.835	0.990	0.882	0.273
	(0.256)	(0.171)	(0.299)	(0.202)	(0.249)	(0.725)
External volatility		0.253				
		(0.543)				
Government size			−0.197			
			(0.830)			
Political constraints				0.582		
				(0.600)		
Investment share					0.272	
					(0.642)	
Financial development						0.060
						(0.024)**
Observations	90	88	90	88	90	78
Adjusted R^2	0.311	0.312	0.304	0.304	0.306	0.398

Note: Numbers in parentheses are robust p-values. Significance levels are *10%; **5%; ***1%. All regressions include a constant. All variables are period differences.

Figure 2.9. Partial Scatter Plots of the Growth Differential Against Differentials in Selected Variables

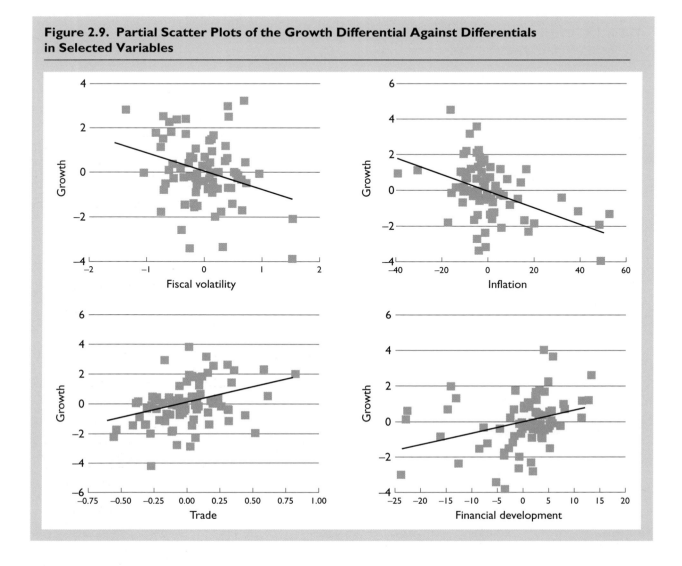

Table 2.6. Decomposition of Turkey's 20-Year Growth Differential

	Estimated Coefficients[1]	Changes in Variables	Growth Contributions (in percent of GDP)
Fiscal volatility	−0.84	0.57	−0.48
Inflation	−0.04	15.77	−0.70
Trade	2.17	1.08	2.35
Initial GDP	−2.50	0.47	−1.17
Financial development	0.06	7.59	0.46

[1]The coefficients are based on the specification (6) in Table 2.5 excluding the Turkey dummy, with virtually identical R-squared and levels of significance.

with an increase in growth by 2.35 percentage points, and (ii) financial development, proxied by growth in the M2/GDP ratio, associated with an increase in growth of .46 percentage point.

Trade therefore was the main component in keeping Turkey's growth constant, as opposed to decreasing as the global average did. If Turkey had also kept inflation and fiscal volatility at the 1960–80 levels, it would have grown almost 1.2 percentage points faster, or about 3.5 percent annually during 1981–2000, about the same rate as the rapidly growing East Asian economies. In cumulative terms, Turkey's GNP would have then been about 27 percent higher in 2000 than it actually turned out to be. In contrast, if macro instability had increased as it did, but trade and financial sector reforms had not occurred, Turkish growth could have been below that of sub-Saharan Africa.

To consider the possibility that the dynamics of growth changed in the 1990s, the sample was divided into decadal averages and the same regression as above was run for decadal growth differences. The results are consistent with those from the 20–year difference regressions, but allow for decomposing the sources of growth on a decadal basis, thereby providing a richer picture of growth developments in Turkey. With three observations per country (for three changes in decadal growth rates between 1960 and 2000), a panel regression was run that included time dummies for the 1980s and the 1990s. The coefficients obtained were then applied to Turkey's actual outcomes of the variables under consideration. Table 2.7 summarizes the calculations.

Growth in trade had overall positive effects on growth, but those effects were most pronounced in the 1980s, when the trend in trade growth appears to have permanently increased. The regress in financial development in the 1970s reduced growth, but its recovery, mostly in the 1980s but also the 1990s, accounted for a significant increase in growth.

While fiscal volatility has a negative effect on the level of growth, the reduction in Turkey's fiscal volatility in the 1990s helped improve growth outcomes relative to the 1980s. However, as Table 2.6 shows, that improvement was not sufficient to overcome the negative effects over 1981–2000 as a whole. Ever-increasing inflation during the three time periods continuously reduced growth. Overall, the results appear to support the assumption that the 1980s were a structural break period, with big growth effects during the decade but smaller growth effects afterwards.

Channels of Growth

Linking the cross-country regressions back to the growth accounting exercise requires examining the channels through which the growth determinants acted. Table 2.8 shows that total factor productivity

growth was hurt mainly by high inflation and helped by financial development. Investment was reduced in countries with high fiscal volatility. Thus, while the determinants of foreign direct investment (FDI) are not explicitly considered, these results offer a perspective on the low levels of FDI in Turkey.

Presumably, macro instability hurt both domestic and foreign investment.[10] Investment increased, however, in the context of more open trade flows, consistent with evidence reported by Wacziarg and Welch (2003). The findings here are inconsistent with micro studies (Ozler and Yilmaz, 2004) that find that TFP increases more rapidly during periods of trade liberalization, although the finding here is that trade liberalization has a stronger impact through investment.

Sources of Policy Volatility

The analysis above leads to the conclusion that further liberalization to improve economic incentives for entrepreneurship, when combined with efforts to reduce fiscal indiscipline, should dramatically improve Turkey's growth outlook. Such an optimistic conclusion would not be warranted if liberalization were accompanied by economic losses for some who could make a political claim on scarce fiscal resources. The consequent effort to make them whole might then have led to bursts of discretionary fiscal expenditures, which would have increased the fiscal deficit while also generating macro volatility. It is possible, for example, that Turkey's remarkable trade liberalization was possible in the first place only through increased discretionary fiscal policy to compensate those who lost from increased openness (several authors have suggested this, especially Waterbury, 1992). While it is not possible to fully explore this question here, the determinants of fiscal volatility can be briefly addressed.

Table 2.9 shows that fiscal volatility is high principally in countries with weak political checks and balances. Thus, more political constraints on executive authority reduce fiscal volatility. Similarly, a presidential form of government, traditionally thought to be more decisive in actions but less constrained, is associated with higher volatility. Notice, though, that the dummy variable for Turkey in the more volatile second period is positive and significant when these conventional measures of political checks and balances are used. Indeed, when the dummy variable for the presidential form of government is added, the Turkey

---

[10]Dutz, Us, and Yilmaz (2005) argue that while macroeconomic instability was the single most important deterrent to foreign direct investment, the perception by foreigners that they may not face a level playing field also limited FDI. They suggest that strengthening the competition policy regime and increasing transparency in bureaucratic processes might help.

Table 2.7. Decomposition of Turkey's Decadal Growth Differentials

	Estimated Coefficients[1]	Changes in Variables			Growth Contributions (in percent of GDP)		
		1970s	1980s	1990s	1970s	1980s	1990s
Fiscal volatility	−0.702	n.a.	0.72	−0.29	n.a.	−0.51	0.20
Inflation	−0.033	17.44	7.39	11.04	−0.58	−0.24	−0.36
Trade	1.786	0.44	0.80	0.35	0.79	1.43	0.63
Initial GDP	−3.993	0.31	0.16	0.26	−1.24	−0.64	−1.04
Financial development	0.120	−8.95	7.84	2.48	−1.08	0.94	0.30

[1]The coefficients were estimated by regressing changes in decadal growth on decadal changes in the explanatory variables plus time dummies. The adjusted R-squared was .425, and all coefficients except the dummy for the 1990s were significant at the 5 percent level or better.

Table 2.8. Cross-Country Difference Regressions with Assorted Dependent Variables

	GDP		TFP		INV	
	(1)	(2)	(3)	(4)	(5)	(6)
Fiscal volatility	−0.959	−0.850	−0.505	−0.420	−0.178	−0.161
	(0.006)***	(0.022)**	(0.195)	(0.292)	(0.038)**	(0.071)*
Inflation	−0.038	−0.045	−0.034	−0.035	−0.003	−0.003
	(0.000)***	(0.000)***	(0.001)***	(0.000)***	(0.269)	(0.268)
Initial per capita GDP	−2.292	−2.500	−2.203	−2.483	−0.081	−0.074
	(0.000)***	(0.000)***	(0.000)***	(0.000)***	(0.409)	(0.518)
Trade openness	2.188	2.128	1.119	1.014	0.639	0.641
	(0.004)***	(0.003)***	(0.100)*	(0.109)	(0.000)***	(0.001)***
Turkey dummy	0.870	0.273	0.231	−0.525	−0.042	−0.088
	(0.256)	(0.725)	(0.725)	(0.410)	(0.798)	(0.604)
Financial development		0.060		0.090		0.003
		(0.024)**		(0.001)***		(0.654)
Observations	90	78	71	62	90	78
Adjusted R^2	0.311	0.398	0.264	0.360	0.172	0.166

Note: Numbers in parentheses are robust p-values. Significance levels are *10%; **5%; ***1%. All regressions include a constant. GDP and total factor productivity are differences in growth rates, INV is the difference in the log of the investment share.

dummy increases in size. The implication is that, although Turkey has had a parliamentary form of government, it has not benefited from the checks and balances inherent in such a system.

For the second period, 1980–2000, there is also a measure of political risk,[11] and the finding is that more political instability is associated with more fiscal volatility. Moreover, the Turkish dummy becomes statistically insignificant. Thus, although constitutional arrangements and political institutions create a legal basis for con-

trolling excessive executive discretion, the workings in practice of the relevant institutions limit the scope for exercising restraint. Several factors may be at work here. Önis (2004) argues that in the interest of moving rapidly ahead with much needed reforms, there was a tendency in Turkey to adopt a Latin American presidential style of decision making, disregarding the legal checks and balances and creating ad hoc bureaucratic structures that weakened the traditional bureaucracy and introduced possibilities for political corruption. At the same time, weak governments consisting of multiparty coalitions and facing frequent elections also had the incentive to patronize their electoral supporters and abandon fiscal discipline. In particular, the agricultural

[11]The political risk measure can take on values between 0 and 100, whereby higher values are associated with lower political risk.

Table 2.9. Cross-Country Fiscal Volatility Regressions
(Dependent variable is log discretionary fiscal volatility)

	1961–1980			1981–2000			
	(1)	(2)	(3)	(4)	(5)	(6)	(7)
Political constraints	−1.508	−1.531	−0.953	−1.735	−1.749	−1.123	
	−(0.000)***	−(0.000)***	−(0.004)***	−(0.000)***	−(0.000)***	(0.074)*	
Presidential			0.514			0.599	
			(0.012)**			(0.030)**	
Trade openness		0.097	0.212		0.141	0.410	0.337
		(0.447)	(0.167)		(0.286)	−(0.006)***	(0.011)**
Political risk[1]							−0.044
							−(0.000)***
Turkey dummy	−0.189	−0.059	0.406	0.498	0.560	1.002	0.155
	(0.004)***	(0.735)	(0.076)*	(0.000)***	(0.000)***	(0.000)***	(0.090)*
Observations	90	90	51	90	90	51	82
Adjusted R^2	0.434	0.432	0.355	0.435	0.437	0.412	0.596

Note: Numbers in parentheses are robust p-values. Significance levels are *10%; **5%; ***1%. All regressions include a constant.
[1]Political risk component from the International Country Risk Guide (ICRG) index average from 1984–2000.

sector and wage earners had to be repeatedly compensated for electoral advantage (Waterbury, 1992).

If trade openness is used as a proxy for the broader liberalization effort undertaken since 1980, it is not associated by itself with higher fiscal volatility. However, once political instability is controlled for, more trade openness since 1980 is associated with greater fiscal discretion and volatility. Thus, controlling for the basic political decision-making structure, reflected in the nature of constraints on executive power, there is some plausibility to the idea that "paying off" constituencies that did not directly benefit from trade was necessary to sustain liberalization. This idea is related to—but different from—one suggested by Rodrik (1999), who argues that more openness creates the need to shield the economy from external shocks and hence requires a bigger government. The suggestion here is instead that more openness may actually bring growth benefits to some but losses to others who need to be compensated.

Looking ahead, then, the lesson is not to restrict the scope for economic liberalization but to strengthen the political institutions that limit harmful discretion. In this regard, Turkey appears to be on a positive trend, including institutional developments as measured, for example, by political constraints. Additional steps in the form of fiscal rules and other measures that impose self-discipline could help in the long term.

Conclusions

Over the past four decades, Turkey experienced several stretches of rapid growth but then relinquished its gains during periodic crises. The result was a solid rather than what could have been a spectacular growth performance. The Turkish story demonstrates the country's entrepreneurial potential for significant growth. Trade and financial sector liberalization in 1980 opened up new opportunities to which the private sector responded energetically, creating a modern and, in some instances, world-class industrial base. These reforms, and the resulting dramatic increase in external trade, were thus key to helping Turkey avoid the secular decline in growth rates that affected most of the rest of the world. Absent these liberalization initiatives, Turkey would likely have grown at rates similar to those of the worst performers in the sample, the sub-Saharan countries.

However, Turkey could have done better than it did. Without deterioration in fiscal and monetary management, Turkey might well have reached growth rates on the order of those found among the best performers in the sample, the rapidly growing East Asian economies.

For Turkey, the crucial question now is whether the forces generating growth can be retained—and bolstered—while those uncertainties inimical to growth are scaled back. Arguably, while the private sector responded in the manner expected by the architects of the reform, the architects' vision of the role of the government proved to be misguided. It was expected that competing demands on limited fiscal resources would be resolved by higher growth and, to this end, the government would further contribute to growth through public investments (Önis and Reidel, 1993). Under this benign vision of the operation of the government, it was considered appropriate to incur debt, which would be paid off by higher rates of growth (Anand, Chhibber, and van Wijnbergen, 1988). However, in practice, government expenditures appear to have been ultimately directed in large measure by the short electoral cycles and the need to maintain the constituent base in the context of weak coalition governments.

The lesson is that sustained growth will require continued structural reforms—including those related to the financial system, corporate governance, and labor markets—to create new avenues for private entrepreneurship as the impetus to growth from earlier liberalization tapers off. At the same time, limiting macro uncertainties will remain crucial. The prognosis on this latter score appears to be an optimistic one, reflected in the recent steady decline in inflation rates. Maintaining this commitment will ultimately require political discipline, which may be helped by fiscal and monetary rules that are not easy to reverse.

III   Turkey's Inflation Process

Oya Celasun and Donal McGettigan

Turkey has had a long history of persistently high inflation. Inflation started to take off during the 1970s and peaked at more than 100 percent in the mid-1990s. Following an unsuccessful exchange rate–based disinflation attempt in 2000–01, inflation did not decline until only recently, under a money-based stabilization program (Figure 3.1). Against this backdrop, this chapter analyzes the reasons behind Turkey's successful disinflation of recent years. Building on earlier work, the chapter finds that inflation expectations—rather than backward-looking indexation mechanisms—dominate price-setting behavior, and have increased in importance in recent years.[1] It also finds that inflation expectations are in turn heavily influenced by fiscal variables.

The Importance of Inflation Expectations

A structural price-setting model is used to test the importance of inflation expectations. Following Gali and Gertler (1999) and Celasun, Gelos, and Prati (2003), a model that nests two types of price-setting behavior is used. Backward-looking agents are assumed to update prices by the most recently observed inflation rate, while forward-looking price setters use current and expected future pricing conditions, particularly real marginal costs. This results in the following equation for inflation dynamics for the inflation rate in period t, π_t:

$$\pi_t = \alpha + \delta^b \pi_{t-1} + \delta^f E_t \pi_{t+1} + \beta mc_t + u_t, \qquad (1)$$

where $\delta^f + \delta^b = 1$, $E_t\pi_{t+1}$ denotes expected inflation in period $t + 1$ in period t, mc_t denotes real marginal costs, α, δ, and β are unknown parameters, and u_t is the disturbance term.

The model is estimated through early 2004 to capture recent progress on disinflation, and is based on 12-month consumer price index (CPI) inflation over

the period from 1995:01 to 1994:02 (see equation 2 below). Real marginal costs are proxied with the real effective exchange rate, given the importance of imported inputs. Inflation expected one year ahead is obtained from survey findings of Consensus Economics, an international economic survey organization, and the Central Bank of Turkey. The estimation frequency is monthly or bimonthly, depending on the frequency at which one-year-ahead inflation is observed. Since the level of the real exchange rate is endogenous to the current disturbance to inflation, u_t, the equation is estimated by two-stage least squares, using the real exchange rate in the previous year, the price of public sector wholesale prices relative to the CPI in the previous year, and current external demand (the GNP of industrialized trade partners) as instruments for the real effective exchange rate.[2]

$$\pi_t = 0.201 - 0.014\pi_{t-1}$$
$$\underset{(0.043***)}{} \quad \underset{(0.079)}{}$$

$$+ 0.914 E_t \pi_{t+1} + 0.584 rer_t. \qquad (2)$$
$$\underset{(0.096***)}{} \quad \underset{(0.167***)}{}$$

The following key findings emerge:
- Inflation expectations dominate the price-setting process. The coefficient of expected future inflation is highly significant, and statistically indistinguishable from 1. In contrast, the coefficient of past inflation is statistically indistinguishable from zero. The real effective exchange rate is also estimated to have a statistically significant coefficient, suggesting that the evolution of foreign prices (measured in domestic currency terms) is a significant determinant of Turkish prices. These findings are not altered when the coefficients of lagged and expected future inflation are constrained to add up to 1—a model restriction that is not rejected in the unconstrained version.
- Inflation expectations have become more important over the estimation period. Recursive estimates are used for samples ending at the start of

---

[1]An earlier version of a similar analysis, which includes more detailed technical discussions, can be found in Celasun, Gelos, and Prati (2003).

[2]The real exchange rate and the GNP of industrialized trade partners deviate from a trend estimated for 1990:01 to 2004:01.

Figure 3.1. Inflation: The Long View
(In percent)

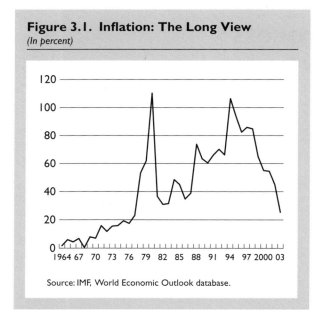

Source: IMF, World Economic Outlook database.

Figure 3.2. Recursive Coefficients of Equation (1)
(Recursive two-stage least squares estimates using annual inflation data)

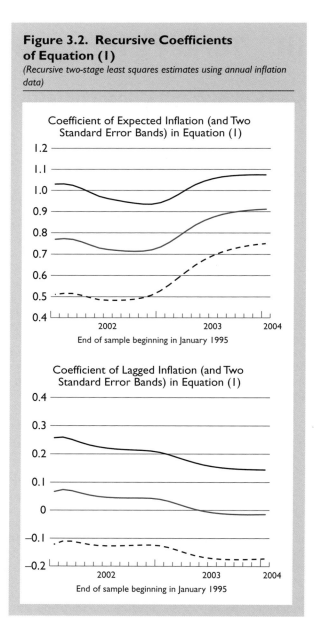

Coefficient of Expected Inflation (and Two Standard Error Bands) in Equation (1)

End of sample beginning in January 1995

Coefficient of Lagged Inflation (and Two Standard Error Bands) in Equation (1)

End of sample beginning in January 1995

the current program supported by the International Monetary Fund right through to early 2004 (Figure 3.2). The coefficient of the real exchange rate is kept fixed to economize on degrees of freedom, but no restrictions are imposed on the lagged and expected future inflation coefficients. The main finding—that the estimated weight on expected future inflation increases while that on past inflation diminishes over time—is robust to allowing the coefficient on the real exchange rate to also vary with the sample, but the confidence bands on the estimates are considerably wider in this case.

- The results are found to be robust when allowance is made for shorter-duration price contracts. If the duration of price contracts is less than one year—quite possible in a country with high and persistent inflation up until recently—the use of quarterly, as opposed to 12-month, inflation measures is a useful robustness test (even allowing for the shorter period of availability of quarterly inflation expectations data and their inherent noisiness).[3,4] The

---

[3]Expectations of one-quarter-ahead inflation are constructed using monthly inflation expectations surveyed bimonthly by Consensus Economics for 1998:05 to 2004:02. Consensus Economics has published average monthly inflation expectations for the six months ahead every other month since 1998:05. For any given month t, we construct a three-month ahead inflation forecast as: $(1 + \pi_{t+1})(1 + \pi_{t+2})(1 + \pi_{t+3}) - 1$, where π_s is the consumer price index inflation forecast for month s.

[4]In order to take into account the potential serial correlation of the residuals in the quarterly specification, the equation is estimated with the generalized method of moments.

results are, however, very similar using quarterly inflation, with inflation expectations predominating and becoming more significant over the sample period (Figure 3.3).

These results are also consistent with the limited evidence of indexation in Turkey. While some elements of public price- and wage-setting behavior involve ex post inflation indexation, there is little evidence of widespread indexation in the private sector. Collective wage bargaining is limited, with private sector wage determination adopting flexibly to labor market conditions. Indeed, Shiller (1997) singles out Turkey as a surprising example of a country that has experienced per-

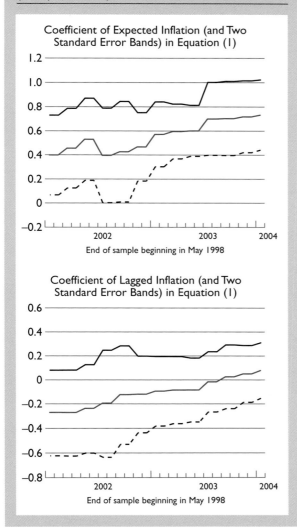

Figure 3.3. Additional Recursive Coefficients of Equation (1)
(Recursive generalized methods of moments estimates using quarterly inflation data)

Coefficient of Expected Inflation (and Two Standard Error Bands) in Equation (1)

End of sample beginning in May 1998

Coefficient of Lagged Inflation (and Two Standard Error Bands) in Equation (1)

End of sample beginning in May 1998

sistently high inflation without moving to widespread indexation.

What Determines Inflation Expectations?

With inflation expectations dominating the price-setting process, anchoring expectations is crucial for successful disinflation. The role of the central bank is key in this respect, with operational independence, a transparent monetary policy, and a clear anchor all playing important roles. But can other factors play a supporting role?

Regression results indicate that fiscal policy can help support the disinflation process by anchoring inflation expectations. To test the role of fiscal policy, a multivariate regression of expected one-year-ahead inflation is run on the primary balance. The regression includes control variables such as past inflation, the exchange rate, short-term money market rates, the real effective exchange rate, and real unit labor costs. The estimation results confirm a strong negative link between expected inflation and the primary balance (Table 3.1). While past inflation is also important, its coefficient is well below 1, suggesting little evidence of a rigidly adaptive expectation formation process. Not surprisingly, exchange rate movements and labor costs also play an important role in driving inflation expectations.[5]

Recursive regressions are used to evaluate the evolving impact in recent years of the following key variables (Figure 3.4):

- *Lagged inflation.* Price setters appear to place a higher weight on lagged inflation in forming price expectations when the inflation path is relatively stable; the opposite holds in periods of uncertainty. For instance, the coefficient on lagged inflation is estimated to have declined sharply during the postcrisis period. This is not surprising, given the uncertainties following the forced float in February 2001, when past manifestations of inflation might not have been expected to convey much information about future inflation trends. In contrast, the weight attached to past inflation increased during periods of relatively predictable disinflation (for instance, beginning in early 2002 as the disinflation process began to take hold).

- *Fiscal outcomes.* The impact of fiscal outcomes is significant for most of the sample period, but was at its highest in 2000, accompanying a sizable improvement in the primary balance. The apparently nonlinear effect of the primary balance on expected inflation suggests that primary fiscal balances play an important signaling role, with large fiscal adjustments signaling the commitment of the government to fiscal sustainability, which in turn curbs inflationary expectations. This is consistent with the fact that the primary balance is significantly linked to inflationary expectations during periods of disinflation from chronically high inflation rates (Celasun, Gelos, and Prati, 2004).

---

[5]The coefficients on these two variables are negative, which is surprising. A possible explanation is that price setters expect reversals in these variables at the annual frequency. If marginal costs have been above trend in a given 12-month period, below-trend marginal costs are expected in the year ahead, leading to lower inflationary expectations.

Table 3.1. Determinants of Inflationary Expectations

Variable	Dependent Variable: Expected Inflation (12-month ahead) Sample: 1995:01–2004:01		
	Coefficient	Std. error	t-statistic
Constant	0.172	0.040	4.233***
Inflation(−2)	0.498	0.059	8.392***
Primary balance/GDP (−2)	−2.485	0.698	−3.557***
Exchange rate depreciation (−2)	0.222	0.033	6.725***
Money market interest rate (−4) − inflation (−4)	−0.0003	0.0009	−0.375
Real exchange rate (−2)	−0.0574	0.2269	−2529**
Real unit labor cost (−2)	−0.128	0.052	−2.488*
Number of observations:	90		
Adjusted R^2	0.90		

Notes: All variables cover a 12-month period. Expected inflation is from Consensus Economics for 1995:01–2001:07, and from the Central Bank of Turkey Survey from 2001:08–2004:01. The difference between the money market rate and inflation, as well as the real exchange rate and the real unit labor cost index (both detrended) are 12-month averages. All variables are lagged (at least two months) to minimize potential endogeneity, and to ensure that the relevant data is available when the expectation is formed. The estimation method is two-stage least squares; the instrument set comprises all regressors except the primary balance, capital expenditures in GDP (−2) (for the consolidated budget), industrialized trade partners' GDP, an index of unit value of imports (−2), the average of the index of crude oil prices over the past 12 months (−2), and the average U.S. government one-year bond rate (−2).

- *Exchange rate.* The exchange rate is estimated to have a statistically insignificant coefficient in samples ending before 2003, but its weight has increased significantly since then. These results suggest that the strong Turkish lira played an important role in aiding the disinflation process in 2003.

Conclusions and Challenges

Turkey's inflation process is quite flexible, with inflation expectations playing a large and increasingly important role in determining inflation rates. This suggests that disinflation need not be too costly as long as inflation expectations are properly anchored. While central bank credibility plays a key role in anchoring these expectations—a topic not addressed here—the chapter suggests that fiscal variables play an important supporting role.

Looking ahead, an important unresolved issue is whether disinflation will become more difficult with

Figure 3.4. Determinants of Inflationary Expectations: Recursive Coefficients
(Recursive two-stage least squares estimates)

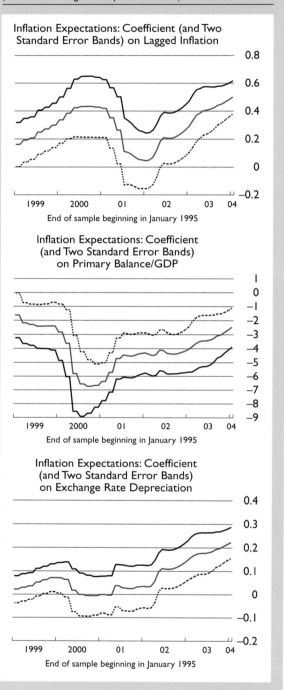

inflation moving to single digits. A possible hint of this is suggested by the fact that past inflation appeared to play a larger role in the formation of expectations under stable conditions. The examination of cross-country evidence for similar disinflation episodes elsewhere may offer useful lessons and will be the subject of future research. For now, at least, inflation inertia does not appear to be a major obstacle to further disinflation. As long as central bank credibility and fiscal discipline are maintained, Turkey should be in a position to continue with its disinflation objectives.

IV Balance Sheet Developments Since the Crisis

Christian Keller and Chris Lane

Following what is called a "balance sheet approach," this chapter assesses the effect of the 2001 crisis on Turkey's main economic sectors, the role those sectors played in resolving the crisis, and how they have developed since then. The approach, which is described by Allen and others (2002),[1] focuses on currency and maturity mismatches in the economy's main sectors and the links between these sectors. Other balance sheet aspects such as the capital structure and off–balance sheet activities are also taken into account to the extent that information is available.

Turkey's 2000–01 financial crisis affected balance sheets throughout the economy. The sharp depreciation that followed the floating of the Turkish lira in February 2001, inflicted heavy net worth losses on balance sheets with large currency mismatches (foreign currency liabilities vs. lira assets). Similarly, the related hike in real interest rates caused financial losses for those who had a maturity mismatch (short-term liabilities vs. long-term assets). Indeed, many banks became insolvent in 2001 as their balance sheets combined large maturity mismatches with large open foreign currency positions. While the crisis initially manifested itself in the banking sector, the related asset price corrections affected balance sheets in all sectors of the economy: the government, banks, corporations, and households.

The resolution of the crisis after mid-2001 brought significant shifts in the sectoral asset-liability positions— mainly transferring risks to the government. To resolve the banking crisis, the government issued bonds with a maturity, interest rate, and currency structure that improved the risk exposure of banks' balance sheets. At the same time, the government used official external financing to provide foreign currency liquidity to the market, as the crisis forced banks and corporations to sharply reduce their outstanding external liabilities. Overall, these transactions meant a reallocation of risks from private balance sheets to those of the government.

The economic recovery in 2002–03 supported a general strengthening of balance sheets. However, certain vulnerabilities remain. Against the backdrop of strong growth, rapid disinflation, and the related improvement in market sentiment, balance sheets in all sectors showed signs of strengthening over 2002 and 2003. That said, some of the vulnerabilities that resulted from the crisis—particularly the level and composition of public debt, and some vulnerabilities that stem from longer-term developments over the past, such as the high level of dollarization in the economy— will require more time to improve.

This chapter first examines how the crisis has impacted Turkey's asset-liability position vis-à-vis non-residents for the country as a whole and the three main sectors: banks, government (including the central bank), and the real sector (households and corporations). Second, because a large portion of domestic liabilities is denominated in foreign currency, there is more detailed analysis of the potential currency and maturity mismatches in each of these sectors. The chapter then highlights the key financial links between the sectors and the vulnerabilities associated with these links. Finally, some policies that could contribute to further strengthening of balance sheets are sketched out.

The Effect of Crisis and Recovery on External Assets and Liabilities

The 2001 crisis temporarily cut Turkey's overall net indebtedness vis-à-vis the rest of the world. But at the sectoral level, the government increased its net external indebtedness, while the banking and the real sectors reduced theirs. At the same time, repayments of short-term external debt over 2001–02, and the accumulation of reserves, led to an improvement of the short-term external asset-liability position of all sectors.

Turkey's net claims on the rest of the world—its international investment position (IIP)—temporarily improved as a result of the 2001 crisis. Key factors in the improvement were the net repayment of external debt (net capital outflow) and, owing to the devaluation, a reduction

---

[1]The term "balance sheet" is not applied in a strict accounting sense but is used to highlight the focus of the approach on financial asset and liability positions (stocks) in addition to flow variables.

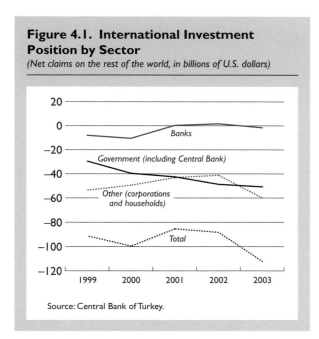

Figure 4.1. International Investment Position by Sector

(Net claims on the rest of the world, in billions of U.S. dollars)

Source: Central Bank of Turkey.

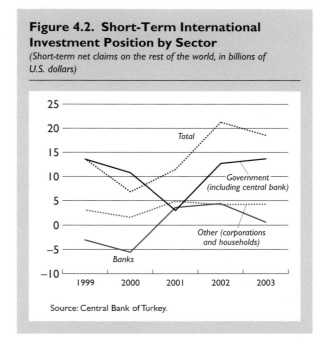

Figure 4.2. Short-Term International Investment Position by Sector

(Short-term net claims on the rest of the world, in billions of U.S. dollars)

Source: Central Bank of Turkey.

in the dollar value of foreign investors' equity position (principally foreign direct investment) in Turkey. The subsequent deterioration reflected a reversal of the capital outflow as well as an upward revaluation of equity assets.

The crisis and the policies to resolve it resulted in major shifts within the country's IIP—improving the banking and real sectors, while weakening the government sector. Turkey's open capital account has long facilitated the extensive use of foreign credit in all sectors. The crawling peg regime adopted in 1999, coupled with high domestic interest rates, further raised incentives for banks and corporations to run large negative IIPs. When the sustainability of the exchange rate peg was called into question, foreign creditors reduced the rollover of their credit, forcing a reduction of the external debt of banks and corporations. To address the risk of widespread banking and corporate default, the government sector responded by (i) selling foreign exchange to the market, (ii) swapping lira paper held by banks for foreign currency-linked bonds, (iii) issuing recapitalization bonds to banks, and (iv) introducing a deposit guarantee. To have the necessary foreign currency liquidity to support these actions, the government borrowed substantially from (official) external creditors. Thus, while the IIP of banks and corporations improved, that of the public sector worsened (Figure 4.1).

The shift across the sectors' short-term IIPs was even more marked. During the crisis, the government sector lost most of its liquid foreign assets (mainly reserves), which worsened the gap between liquid foreign assets and short-term foreign liabilities. In contrast, both banks and corporations built a positive short-term IIP: the for-

eign credit they lost had been mostly short term, and at the same time, they accumulated liquid foreign assets as part of a strengthening of the current account. However, by 2002, the public sector position had also begun to strengthen markedly as the need for foreign exchange intervention ended and longer-term finance from the International Monetary Fund bolstered reserves (Figure 4.2).

However, given the extensive dollarization of domestic liabilities in Turkey, foreign assets and liabilities are only a part of the foreign currency risk in each sector. In total, more than half of all debt liabilities in Turkey, including those between residents, are denominated in foreign currency. This so-called domestic liability dollarization can substantially affect a sector's overall foreign currency exposure beyond the position it has vis-à-vis nonresidents.[2] For example, despite the positive short-term IIP described above, the banking sector still has a large mismatch between its short-term foreign currency assets and liabilities because of the large share of residents' foreign currency deposits. Similarly, foreign currency-denominated loans received from domestic banks can substantially add to the foreign currency liabilities of corporations. Although these liabilities among residents in principle net out when aggregated on the country level (the IIP for Turkey as a whole), they can still cause distress in

---

[2]The term "foreign currency position" refers to the position including domestic assets and liabilities that are denominated in or indexed to a foreign currency.

Table 4.1. Extent of Liability Dollarization in Turkey's Economy, end-2003

(In billions of U.S. dollars)

	Government Sector	Banking Sector	Real Sector[1]	Total
Total debt	203	153	88	444
Foreign currency debt	94	77	61	232
of which domestic	31	57	22	109
Foreign currency debt as percent of total	46	50	70	52

Source: IMF staff calculations based on data from the Banking Regulation and Supervision Agency and the Central Bank.

[1]The real sector's total debt is the sum of its external debt and its credit from domestic banks.

Figure 4.3. Foreign Currency Share in Total Debt, end-2002

(In percent)

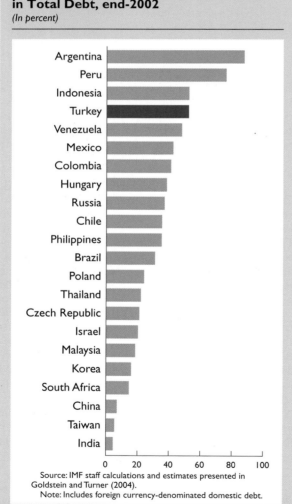

Source: IMF staff calculations and estimates presented in Goldstein and Turner (2004).

Note: Includes foreign currency-denominated domestic debt.

sectoral balance sheets and be a source of economic disruption (Table 4.1 and Figure 4.3).

Resolution of the Crisis and Recovery of Balance Sheets in Each Sector

Banking Sector

Large foreign currency mismatches combined with significant maturity mismatches had been a key weakness that contributed to the crisis many banks experienced in 2001. With bonds provided by the government, banks have since been able to recapitalize and reduce their currency and interest rate exposure. However, some vulnerabilities associated with the high share of foreign currency deposits remain, and banks are also highly exposed to government assets.

The foreign currency mismatch in the banking sector has been dramatically reduced since the crisis.[3] The banking sector's open foreign currency position, including forwards, was reduced from more than $5 billion at end-2000 (40 percent of total shareholder equity including profits) to a slightly positive position by end-2003.[4] This adjustment, which greatly reduces the sector's exchange rate risk, was the result of three main developments:

- Banks repaid their foreign interbank credit lines during the crisis. Short-term credit from foreign banks fell from almost $17 billion in 2000 to $8 billion in 2001, which translated into an improvement in the on-balance sheet foreign currency position (excluding foreign currency-indexed assets) of about $7 billion.

---

[3]The banking sector comprises private, state, Savings Deposit Insurance Fund, and foreign and investment banks.

[4]Banks' forward positions are netted out for the purpose of calculating the regulatory limit.

Table 4.2. Foreign Currency Mismatch in the Banking Sector
(In billions of U.S. dollars)

		1999	2000	2001	2002	2003
1	On-balance sheet currency mismatch (excluding foreign currency indexed assets)	−7.0	−17.7	−10.1	−9.7	−9.2
2	Foreign currency indexed assets	...	3.4	8.6	9.1	9.2
3=1+2	On-balance sheet currency mismatch	...	−14.3	−1.6	−0.6	0.0
4	Forward position	...	9.1	1.5	0.1	0.3
5=3+4	Currency mismatch (including forwards)	...	−5.2	−0.1	−0.4	0.3
Memo item: Short-term credit from foreign banks		13.2	16.9	8.0	6.3	9.7

Source: IMF staff calculations based on data from the Banking Regulation and Supervision Agency and the Central Bank of Turkey.

- Foreign currency-indexed assets jumped from $3.5 billion in 2000 to $8.6 billion in 2001, which was mainly the result of a swap of about $5 billion worth of lira-denominated government debt to dollar-linked bonds in June 2001. This reduced the gap between foreign currency assets and liabilities to $1.6 billion.
- Owing to these two drastic improvements in their on-balance sheet position, banks were able to wind down their very large long-forward position—from over $9 billion in 2000 to only about $1.5 billion in 2001—and still reduce their overall currency mismatch to just a little above $100 million (Table 4.2).[5]

With the maturity of deposits remaining very short, banks continue to have a significant maturity mismatch, to a large extent in foreign currency. The banking system did not experience deposit flight during the crisis; in fact, foreign currency deposits continued to increase in 2001. The maturity of deposits, however, has not lengthened significantly despite the resolution of the crisis. The average maturity of less than three months is still very short for both lira and foreign currency deposits. The comparatively longer maturities of the banking sector's assets (both government securities and private sector loans) create a substantial maturity mismatch on bank balance sheets. The issuance of floating rate notes by the government has allowed banks to reduce some of the interest rate risk associated with the maturity gap between deposits and assets.[6] However, the foreign currency liquidity risk resulting from the large

share of short-term foreign currency deposits remains substantial (Figures 4.4 and 4.5).

Banks' liquidity coverage of foreign currency deposits declined during the 2002–03 recovery. Banks generally maintain a higher liquidity coverage for foreign currency deposits than for lira deposits—reflecting the higher risk of intermediating in foreign currency. This coverage has been declining over the past two years, as banks shift out of low-yielding liquid foreign currency assets into longer-term domestic assets with higher yields (such as consumer loans). By end-2003, less than one-third of the $54 billion foreign currency deposits were covered with liquid assets (including banks' reserves at the Central Bank). This indicates an improvement in the banks' financial intermediation function and also their profitability, but, as indicated above, it also heightens liquidity and repricing risk (Figures 4.6 and 4.7).

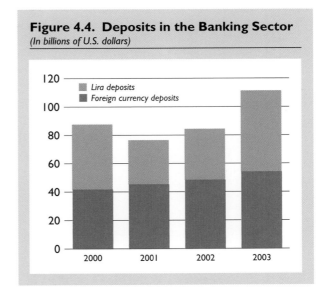

Figure 4.4. Deposits in the Banking Sector
(In billions of U.S. dollars)

---
[5]The quality of forwards as of end-2000 has been an issue of debate. Many observers believe that the counterparts to these contracts often were corporations that did not have sufficient foreign currency earnings to actually fulfill their obligations had the forwards been called.

[6]There is little information on the maturity structure of loans to the private sector. Given the existence of floating rate loans, the maturity and the repricing period might diverge.

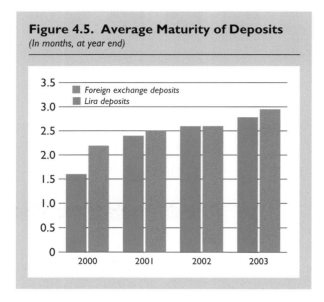

Figure 4.5. Average Maturity of Deposits
(In months, at year end)

Figure 4.7. Government Securities as a Share of the Banking Sector's Total Loan and Security Portfolio
(In percent)

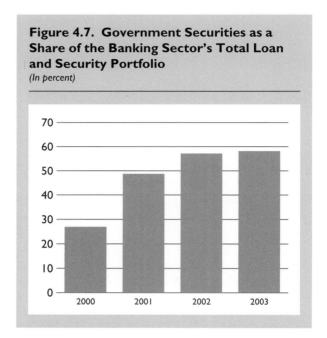

Banks' exposure to government assets has risen sharply as a result of the crisis. The share of government securities in banks' total portfolios of loans and securities about doubled in 2001, reaching 50 percent by year-end. This was the direct result of the government providing banks with bonds to improve their capitalization, and to the government's much increased borrowing requirement due to the hike in real interest rates.

Government Sector

During and immediately after the crisis, the government's balance sheet deteriorated, its debt stock rose,

Figure 4.6. Liquid Assets (including reserves) as a Share of Deposits
(In percent)

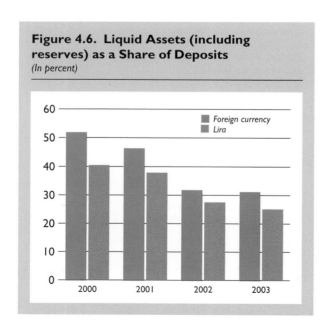

the share of foreign currency debt and floating rate debt increased, maturities shortened, and the net reserve position weakened. Since 2002, with the return of confidence and growth, all of these indicators have begun to improve. But the level and the composition of debt remain a concern.

The most noticeable impact of the crisis on the government's balance sheet was the jump in debt, which largely reflects its involvement in the recapitalization of banks. First, domestic debt soared in 2001 as a result of the government's issuance of securities to recapitalize banks (so-called noncash debt). Second, external debt rose, as credit from the International Monetary Fund increased. Third, the depreciation of the exchange rate and the hike in interest rates greatly increased the government's debt burden (Table 4.3).

The composition of government debt also worsened during the crisis—yet it recovered somewhat in 2002–03 as market conditions improved. The share of government debt denominated in or indexed to foreign currency rose to nearly 60 percent by end-2002, reflecting the onlending of IMF credit from the Central Bank of Turkey and debt issued for bank recapitalization mainly denominated in foreign currency. Floating interest rate debt increased to nearly 70 percent of total debt in 2001, as fixed rate debt issuance carried very high interest rates. As market conditions improved, floating rate debt and foreign currency debt each declined to just under half the debt stock by 2003, underscoring the continued sensitivity of the debt stock to interest rate and exchange rate changes (Table 4.4).

The government's available foreign currency assets fell in 2001 and did not increase enough in 2002–03

Table 4.3. Gross Government Debt (consolidated budget debt stock)
(In billions of U.S. dollars)

	1999	2000	2001	2002	2003
Domestic debt (cash)	37.4	43.8	40.2	54.6	93.5
Domestic debt (noncash)	5.0	10.4	44.7	37.1	45.8
External debt	34.6	39.5	38.8	56.8	63.5
Total	77.0	93.7	123.6	148.5	202.8

Source: IMF staff calculations based on data from the Banking Regulation and Supervision Agency and the Central Bank of Turkey.

to avoid a widening of its currency mismatch. The government's foreign currency position deteriorated markedly, both on a total and short-term basis. Short-term exposure, measured as net reserves less short-term debt on a remaining maturity basis, recovered in 2002 as maturities lengthened, but rose again at end-2003 owing to the shorter maturity of onlent fund credit and debt swaps due in 2004 (Table 4.5).

Real Sector

The crisis forced the real sector as a whole (corporations and households) to a positive foreign currency position during 2001, which it largely retained in 2002–03. However, while households in aggregate are largely hedged through their holdings of foreign currency assets, corporations continue to have a high foreign currency mismatch, and the natural hedge from exports appears limited. Also, the equity cushion of corporations remains small and much of their debt is still short term.

The real sector moved to a large positive foreign currency position by end-2001, as foreign and do-

mestic banks cut their (foreign currency) loans. The real sector typically had a large negative position vis-à-vis nonresidents, reflecting its dependence on external borrowing. At the same time, however, its domestic foreign currency position has been long, because its dollar deposits with domestic banks have been much higher than the amount of dollar loans it receives from these banks (since banks give most of their credit to the government). Taken together, the real sector had a slightly negative foreign currency position at end-2000. During the crisis, both foreign and domestic banks reduced their lending to Turkey's real sector, while the sector maintained most of its foreign asset holdings and domestic dollar deposits. As a result, the real sector's overall foreign currency position swung from an $800 million deficit in 2000 to a $9.6 billion surplus in 2001.

While foreign currency borrowing resumed in 2002–03, the real sector also added to its foreign currency assets, thus retaining a positive foreign currency balance. As access to foreign credit was regained and the domestic banking system recovered, the real sector was again able to take on foreign currency debt in

Table 4.4. Currency and Interest Rate Composition of Central Government Debt
(In percent of total debt)

	1999	2000	2001	2002	2003
External debt	44.9	42.2	31.4	38.3	31.3
Domestic foreign currency debt	...	5.6	24.4	19.8	15.1
of which: indexed	...	3.5	13.5	8.1	6.3
Total foreign currency debt	...	47.7	55.8	58.1	46.4
Debt at variable interest rates[1]	...	49.4	68.5	51.8	48.6

Source: IMF staff calculations based on Treasury data.
[1]Including estimates of floating rate foreign currency debt for 2000 and 2001.

Table 4.5. Foreign Currency Position of the Government Sector
(In billions of U.S. dollars)

	1999	2000	2001	2002	2003
Total foreign currency debt	...	44.7	69.0	86.3	94.0
of which: Domestic foreign currency debt	...	5.2	30.2	29.5	30.5
of which: External debt	34.6	39.5	38.8	56.8	63.5
Central Bank net international reserves (excluding IMF on-lent)		14.4	6.7	15.9	19.7
Foreign currency position (Central Bank + Treasury)	...	−30.3	−62.3	−70.4	−74.3
Short-term foreign currency debt (remaining maturity)[1]		6.7	14.3	14.2	23.3
Short-term foreign currency position[2]		7.7	−7.7	1.7	−3.6

Source: Treasury, Central Bank of Turkey, and IMF staff estimates.

[1]External debt plus estimated data for foreign currency indexed and denominated debt with maturity less than one year. Excludes long-term Dresdner deposits with less than one year remaining.

[2]Central Bank net international reserves less short-term foreign currency debt at remaining maturity.

2002 and 2003. In parallel, it also rebuilt its assets abroad, and, in particular, boosted its foreign currency deposits with domestic banks. Thus, overall, the surplus in the real sector's foreign currency position that had emerged by end-2001 only shrunk by about one-third (to $6.3 billion) in the two years that followed (Table 4.6).

The data indicate, however, that within the real sector, corporations have a currency mismatch, while households have a large foreign currency surplus. Domestic banking sector data show that corporations' deposits account for less than one-quarter of foreign currency deposits, while at the same time the corporations receive about three-quarters of the bank loans. Similarly, households are unlikely to issue external debt, while they are likely to hold a significant share of reported foreign assets. Calculations based on this information reveal a large gap between the foreign currency assets and liabilities on the balance sheets of corporations. Given the real sector's overall surplus,

this implies that households have a very large surplus in their foreign currency position (Table 4.7).

Consequently, households in aggregate seem well hedged against exchange rate risk. The long foreign currency position of households can be explained by the fact that they need less foreign currency financing and at the same time still largely substitute lira assets with foreign currency assets. Hence, while an exchange rate depreciation would still reduce the real value of households' lira wages, it would create a positive wealth effect through their dollar savings.

Corporations have some natural hedge through their ability to generate foreign currency from exports, but this is limited by their need to pay for imported inputs. In contrast to households, whose income is mostly in lira, corporations that produce tradable goods—in the clothing and textiles sector, for example—can generate foreign currency income from exports. This provides them with a natural hedge against currency risk to the extent that an exchange

Table 4.6. Foreign Currency Position of the Real Sector (corporations and households)
(In billions of U.S. dollars)

		1999	2000	2001	2002	2003
1	External debt	−31.7	−34.4	−31.9	−35.6	−39.8
2	Foreign assets	12.2	11.3	12.5	13.7	13.7
3 (=1+2)	External position (all in foreign currency)	−19.5	−23.0	−19.4	−22.0	−26.2
4	Foreign currency loans from domestic banks	...	−19.6	−16.3	−17.8	−21.6
5	Foreign currency deposits with domestic banks	...	41.8	45.3	48.4	54.1
6 (=4+5)	Domestic foreign currency position	...	22.2	29.0	30.5	32.5
7 (=3+6)	Total foreign currency mismatch	...	−0.8	9.6	8.5	6.3

Source: IMF staff calculations based on data from the Banking Regulation and Supervision Agency and the Central Bank of Turkey.

Table 4.7. Foreign Currency Position of the Corporate Sector
(In billions of U.S. dollars)

		1999	2000	2001	2002	2003
1	External debt[1]	−31.7	−34.4	−31.9	−35.6	−39.8
2	Foreign assets[2]	6.1	5.7	6.3	6.8	6.8
3 (=1+2)	External position (all in foreign currency)	−25.6	−28.7	−25.7	−28.8	−33.0
4	Foreign currency loans from domestic banks[3]	. . .	−14.7	−12.2	−13.4	−16.2
5	Foreign currency deposits with domestic banks[4]	. . .	10.4	11.3	12.1	13.5
6 (=4+5)	Domestic foreign currency position	. . .	−4.3	−0.9	−1.3	−2.7
7 (=3+6)	Total foreign currency mismatch	. . .	−32.9	−26.5	−30.1	−35.7

Source: IMF staff calculations based on data from the Banking Regulation and Supervision Agency and the Central Bank of Turkey.

[1]Assuming that all the external private debt is owed by corporations.
[2]Assuming that half of the foreign assets belongs to households.
[3]Assuming that three-fourths of bank loans are extended to corporations.
[4]Assuming that one-fourth of bank deposits belong to corporations.

rate depreciation improves their competitiveness and thus boosts exports. The production of export goods, however, often requires the import of input goods, which are not easily substituted with local goods, and for which corporations must pay in foreign currency. Some estimates indicate that one-half to two-thirds of the value of exported goods in Turkey are imported inputs. For 2001 and 2002, for example, this would imply a net inflow of foreign currency receipts from exports (excluding shuttle trade) of between $12 billion and $16 billion, compared to a foreign currency mismatch of between $26 billion and $30 billion.

Although the available aggregate data show some improvement in the capital structure of corporations since the crisis, debt capital still dominates. In most Turkish corporations, debt financing dominates over equity financing. During the 2001 crisis, the average leverage ratio of corporations increased to about 70 percent,

equivalent to a debt-to-equity ratio of over 230 percent. However, after returning to its precrisis level in 2002, the leverage ratio improved further in 2003 to about 60 percent (debt-to-equity ratio of 150 percent). Although such levels are not uncommon for emerging market economies, they imply that the equity buffer against balance sheet shocks is still limited in most corporations.

Most of corporate debt still has short maturities, however, which creates a large mismatch between the liquid assets and short-term liabilities of corporations. Two-thirds of the debt financing is short term, and only about one-fourth of these short-term liabilities are covered by liquid assets. Although these ratios clearly improved in 2002–03, they still imply that corporations have a significant exposure to interest rate and rollover risk (Table 4.8).

A look at the 2001 income statements of corporations shows how currency and maturity mismatches

Table 4.8. Selected Financial Ratios of the Corporate Sector
(In percent)

	1999	2000	2001	2002	2003
Liquidity					
Current assets/short-term liabilities (current ratio)	117.8	121.1	112.8	122.3	124.8
Liquid assets (including marketable securities)/ short-term liabilities (cash ratio)	25.7	25.6	23.4	26.3	26.3
Financial position					
Total loans/total assets (leverage ratio)	69.4	66.5	70.1	64.6	60.1
Total loans/own funds (debt-to-equity ratio)	226.4	198.5	234.2	182.8	150.8
Short-term liabilities/total liabilities	49.1	47.5	47.8	42.4	41.7
Short-term liabilities/total loans	70.7	71.4	68.2	65.7	69.3

Source: Central Bank of Turkey.

Figure 4.8. Operating and Net Profits of Corporations

(In billions of U.S. dollars)

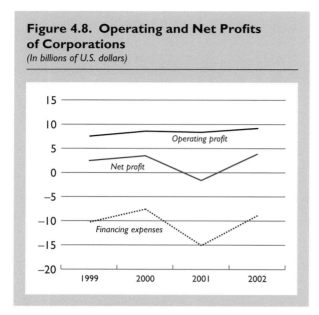

can adversely affect their financial health. Sales numbers for corporations in 2001 show a rise in exports parallel to the collapse in the value of domestic sales, thus confirming some natural hedge effect from the exchange rate depreciation. Since the depreciation of the lira also implied a sharp fall in domestic production costs, corporations were even able to maintain their operating profits in 2001. Given their large share of short-term and foreign currency debt, however, the soaring interest rates and the depreciation of the lira created a spike in financing expenses.

This turned the operating profits into net losses (Figure 4.8 and Table 4.9).

Main Links Between Sectoral Balance Sheets and Associated Risks

To resolve the crisis, risks were transferred from private sector balance sheets to the balance sheet of the government. As a result, the government sector balance sheet now plays a central role in the possible transmission of shocks. An additional risk stems from the still-high share of foreign currency intermediation by banks, which spreads foreign currency liquidity risk into all sectors of the economy and is only partly cushioned by the official reserve position.

The government strengthened the banking sector balance sheet by increasing the level, and worsening the structure, of its own debt. It issued bonds to recapitalize banks and provided foreign currency assets to the rest of the economy to close open foreign currency positions. Banks and corporations had large short-term foreign currency liabilities, and, at the same time, had either completely lost access to foreign credit or could only obtain it at much shorter maturities and higher costs than the official financing that was available to the government (Figure 4.9).

As a result, the government's balance sheet has now become the linchpin for the rest of the economy. Given the increased exposure of banks' balance sheets to government assets, the sustainability of government debt and the health of the banking sector are intimately linked. In turn, because of their financial

Table 4.9. Selected Profitability Ratios of the Corporate Sector

	1999	2000	2001	2002	2003
Relative to capital					
Net profit/own funds	7.5	8.0	0.0	9.4	8.7
Net profit/total assets[1]	2.3	2.7	0.0	3.3	3.5
Relative to sales					
Operating profit/net sales	3.8	2.5	4.0	4.9	3.9
Net profit/net sales[1]	1.2	1.0	0.0	2.2	2.2
Cost of goods sold/net sales	90.5	93.0	91.1	87.8	89.3
Interest expenses/net sales	5.1	2.2	6.5	4.5	2.2
Relative to financial obligations					
Profit before interest and tax/interest expenses (interest coverage ratio)	146.8	182.3	111.1	174.9	251.6
Net profit and interest expenses/ interest expenses	123.8	146.0	96.8	148.0	200.1

Source: Central Bank of Turkey.

[1] Profits in 2001 were negative, but the profitability ratios are reported as zero.

Figure 4.9. Domestic Banking Sector's Claims on Public Sector Assets
(Percent of total assets)

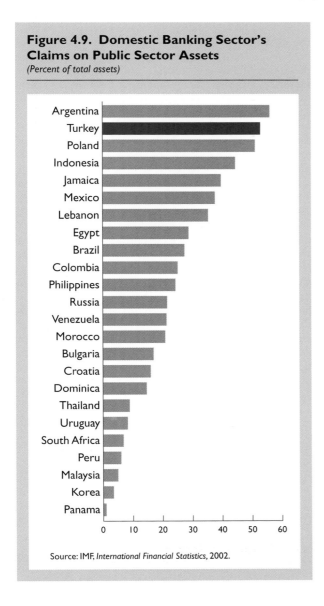

Source: IMF, *International Financial Statistics*, 2002.

Table 4.10. Main Domestic Foreign Currency Assets and Liabilities of the Banking Sector, end-2003
(In billions of U.S. dollars)

	Assets	Liabilities
Resident's foreign currency deposits		54.1
Foreign currency denominated securities (mainly government)	26.4	
Foreign currency denominated loans (mainly private sector)	21.6	
Foreign currency index assets (loans and securities; private and government)	9.2	
Total	57.2	54.1

Source: IMF staff calculations based on data from the Banking Regulation and Supervision Agency.

intermediation function, banks have a strong impact on the stability of the real sector.

The banking sector's lack of funding through lira deposits from the real sector inevitably creates exchange rate or related risks. As shown earlier, households protect their wealth from inflation by converting their mostly lira income into foreign currency assets, mainly in the form of bank deposits. To match the short-term foreign currency liabilities created by these deposits, banks attempt to create domestic foreign currency assets with the government and the real sector: They extend private sector loans and demand government securities that are denominated or indexed in foreign currency. Together, these assets more than matched residents' foreign currency de-

posits by end-2003 (Table 4.10). However, by shifting the exchange rate risk to the government and the real sector, banks increase their exposure to *credit risk*, in that corporations, households, or the government may not be able to serve their foreign currency debt to banks after a sharp exchange rate depreciation; and to *market risk*, in that, because the security portfolio of banks is marked-to-market, any sudden drop in the price of government securities implies a fall in the banks' assets.

The short maturity of most foreign currency liabilities creates a high liquidity risk throughout the economy, which is only in part covered by official reserve assets. Turkey's total short-term external debt (residual maturity basis) amounted to 119 percent of gross official reserves by end-2003. Yet, this traditional reserve adequacy ratio may not fully capture the economy's true foreign currency liquidity risk. Indeed, to better gauge the total foreign currency liquidity needs that could emerge in the economy over the short term, it is useful to add the foreign currency deposits of residents and those of domestic banks (net of the banks' own liquid foreign assets) to the short-term external debt. Measured this way, the potential short-term foreign currency needs add up to over 250 percent of gross reserves. Thus, while gross official reserves are almost high enough to fully cover the economy's foreign currency needs to repay short-term external debt, they do not suffice to also cover the potential foreign currency liquidity needs of banks, should residents suddenly want to withdraw their dollar deposits from the domestic banking system.

Conclusions and Policy Implications

The balance sheet analysis provides a comprehensive perspective for examining the vulnerabilities in Turkey's economy. The results can be summarized as follows:

- Banking sector—Banks' balance sheets have strengthened significantly since 2001, but they are highly exposed to government assets, and foreign currency liquidity risk will also remain as long as dollar deposits are a main funding source.
- Government sector—The government's high and adversely structured debt stock is its main vulnerability. Its ample reserve holdings only partly mitigate the related risks, given the economy's large potential short-term foreign currency needs.
- Real sector—The profitability of corporations has recovered, but the combination of short-term foreign currency debt and still-limited equity capital continues to pose a risk. The large foreign currency holdings (in aggregate) of households hedge them against currency risk.

The findings reinforce the existing policy advice regarding a public debt reduction strategy and the management of foreign currency risks. Lower levels of public debt would reduce the vulnerability not only of the government sector but—given the intersectoral links—also of the banking and real sectors. Limiting the share of foreign currency debt, lengthening the maturity of liabilities, and maintaining prudent levels of liquid foreign currency assets are further steps to reduce balance sheet risks. In addition, policies to promote equity financing could help to decrease corporations' high leverage, which would strengthen their resilience against any type of shock. Continuing trade facilitation will improve the degree to which exports can react to an exchange rate depreciation, thus enabling corporations to better benefit from their natural hedge.

Given the many risks related to domestic liability dollarization, policies that encourage reverse currency substitution are also important. Low inflation and the removal of distortions in financial intermediation should, over the medium term, encourage residents to keep their savings in lira assets. The ability of local banks to fund themselves with lira deposits will allow them to move away from intermediating in foreign currency, which, as shown earlier, lies at the root of the high currency exposure found on balance sheets throughout the economy.

V How Much Debt Is Too Much?

Christoph Klingen

Turkey has made good progress in reducing its public debt ratio since 2001, but the ratio is still high and remains a key source of vulnerability. A strong fiscal effort and the successful stabilization of the exchange rate reduced gross public debt relative to GNP from a peak of 101 percent in 2001 to 79 percent at end-2003. But this debt stock is still large, especially considering the high debt service ratio it implies (175 percent of revenue) and its sensitivity to exchange rate and interest rate changes.

What debt level should Turkey target in the medium term? Before attempting to answer this question, one needs to examine what would constitute a suitable yardstick against which to measure the sustainability, safety, or advisability of the debt position. This chapter surveys the literature for the different yardsticks for assessing public debt. Particular focus is on studies that relate to emerging market economies, with a view to distilling tentative lessons for Turkey. Following a cursory glance at the main features of Turkey's debt, the chapter discusses six methods of assessing public debt:

- *Deterministic debt sustainability.* This staple of fiscal analysis compares the "debt-stabilizing primary surplus" or the "debt threshold" against the actual primary surplus or debt ratio, respectively, to determine whether public debt relative to GNP explodes over time or remains contained.
- *Stochastic debt sustainability.* This approach extends the above deterministic exercise by explicitly recognizing that relevant economic variables like growth, real interest rates, and the exchange rate are subject to shocks. It is therefore necessary to build a safety margin into debt thresholds to ensure that debt remains sustainable should an adverse environment materialize.
- *Fiscal track record approach.* This is another variant of the debt sustainability exercise, but rather than basing the calculations on fiscal targets, it uses primary surplus projections guided by past experience. This approach sets a high bar for sustainability, as it rules out fiscal policy breaking with its past.
- *Empirical debt sustainability.* This is a purely statistical approach that tries to determine which economic variables best explain the onset of sovereign debt distress or dangerously low investor ratings. External debt and debt service ratios, indicators of macroeconomic instability, and credit history are found to be key.
- *Fiscal dominance of monetary policy.* This line of research points to a "default risk channel" in monetary policy. Interest rate policy might have perverse effects in high-debt countries because higher interest rates translate into higher debt service obligations and higher default risk. This triggers capital outflows, currency depreciation, and higher—not lower—inflation. Fiscal dominance is rooted in investors' concerns about debt sustainability.
- *Real interest rates and financial intermediation.* Sustainability considerations aside, high real interest rates and large government claims on the lending capacity of banks are signs in themselves that the government is overborrowing.

Main Features of Turkey's Public Debt

Turkey's public debt grew significantly over the past decade. In gross terms, the debt increased from around 50 percent of GNP in the mid-1990s to about 80 percent of GNP in 2003. In the crisis year of 2001, it peaked at just over 100 percent of GNP (Table 5.1). The large upward jump of the debt ratio in that year reflects the recognition of public debt that had been building up over the years outside the official Treasury debt statistics. It also reflects bank restructuring costs in the wake of the financial crisis, and the capital loss on foreign currency-denominated debt in the aftermath of the exchange rate devaluation. Since then, fiscal adjustment together with exchange rate stabilization have improved the debt ratio.

The structure of the debt entails substantial exchange rate and interest rate risk. Including its external debt, 46 percent of the government's total debt is denominated in, or indexed to, foreign currency (as of end-2003). Consequently, any (real) devaluation of the domestic currency directly translates into a sizable increase in the debt ratio. Moreover, about half of the

Table 5.1. Main Features of Turkey's Debt

(In percent)

	1994	1995	1996	1997	1998	1999	2000	2001	2002	2003
Size of debt										
Net public sector debt/GNP	...	...	...	...	...	...	57.4	90.9	78.6	70.5
Gross Treasury debt/GNP	53.7	42.8	44.2	43.3	40.6	53.1	50.7	100.8	88.2	79.3
Gross Treasury domestic debt/GNP	20.6	17.3	21.0	21.4	21.7	29.3	29.0	69.2	54.5	54.5
Foreign debt/GNP	...	...	42.9	43.5	46.9	55.0	59.0	79.0	71.7	61.8
Foreign Treasury debt/GNP	...	...	23.2	21.9	18.9	23.8	21.7	31.6	33.8	24.8
Government debt relative to servicing capacity										
Net public sector debt/central government revenue	...	...	...	...	...	...	213.6	309.8	283.1	250.8
Net public sector debt/general government revenue	...	...	...	...	...	...	172.4	246.2	223.1	194.6
Gross Treasury debt/central government revenue	...	...	...	...	185.3	221.2	188.5	343.4	317.7	282.2
Gross Treasury debt/general government revenue	...	...	...	...	...	...	152.2	273.0	250.4	219.0
External debt relative to servicing capacity										
External debt/exports	...	...	174.2	162.5	177.4	225.6	232.3	225.8	239.8	215.7
External debt/reserves	...	...	4.8	4.5	4.9	4.4	6.0	6.1	4.9	4.4
Composition of debt										
Share of foreign exchange denominated or indexed debt in gross Treasury debt	...	...	...	...	50.1	47.6	47.0	55.8	58.1	46.4
Share of floating rate instruments in gross Treasury debt	...	...	...	...	...	...	...	...	55.0	51.1
Share of floating rate instruments in gross domestic Treasury debt	...	...	32.1	38.0	31.2	25.8	40.6	76.8	63.7	56.3
Share of gross Treasury debt that is neither floating instrument nor foreign exchange denominated or indexed	...	...	...	...	...	...	...	...	15.5	24.2
Maturity structure of debt										
Average maturity of domestic debt instruments in months (excluding nonmarketable bank recapitalization bonds)	...	...	...	...	4.6	11.7	9.4	19.2	12.8	12.4
Redemptions/end of period Treasury gross debt stock	28.1	39.4	48.3	25.4	42.5	39.3	31.6	35.8	35.9	41.1
Redemptions/GDP	15.1	16.9	21.3	11.0	17.2	20.9	16.0	36.1	31.7	32.6
Redemptions/general government revenue	...	...	...	...	...	...	48.1	97.8	90.0	90.1
Debt servicing costs										
Nominal t-bill rate	...	...	...	...	...	106.2	38.0	99.1	63.5	44.1
Ex-post real rate (GNP deflator)	...	...	...	...	...	32.3	−8.5	28.2	13.7	17.2
EMBI+ spread in basis points	...	...	...	...	...	504	507	883	758	624
EMBI+ spread as multiple of Baa spread	...	...	...	...	...	1.3	1.1	2.7	3.5	3.7
Central government interest bill/GNP	7.7	7.3	10.0	7.7	11.5	13.7	16.3	23.3	18.9	16.4
Central government interest bill/central government revenue	39.9	41.2	55.5	39.4	52.7	57.0	60.6	79.3	67.9	58.5
Treasury debt service/GNP	22.8	24.2	31.3	18.8	28.8	34.6	32.3	59.4	50.6	49.1
Treasury debt service/central government revenue	118.4	136.0	173.8	95.4	131.5	144.0	120.2	202.2	182.0	174.6
Macroeconomic indicators										
Real GDP growth	−0.1	0.1	0.1	8.3	3.9	−6.1	6.3	−9.5	7.8	5.9
Consumer price index inflation (annual average)	106.3	88.0	80.4	85.7	84.6	64.9	54.9	54.4	45.0	25.3
GDP inflation (annual average)	107.3	87.1	77.9	81.2	75.3	55.8	50.9	55.3	43.8	22.9
Nominal depreciation against US$ in percent	63.0	35.0	43.5	46.5	41.8	37.7	33.0	49.1	18.6	−0.6
Real effective depreciation	...	...	2.7	6.5	8.4	3.9	10.9	−17.6	11.4	8.9
Central government revenue/GNP	19.2	17.8	18.0	19.7	21.9	24.0	26.9	29.4	27.8	28.1
Primary surplus/GNP (program definition)	...	...	...	...	...	−0.7	3.0	5.5	4.1	6.2
Central government primary surplus/GNP (Ministry of Finance definition)	3.8	3.3	1.8	0.1	4.4	2.0	5.7	6.8	4.3	5.3
Deposit money banks' assets/GNP	35.4	33.6	36.4	42.8	48.6	63.3	66.7	81.0	64.0	58.7
Deposit money banks claims on government/ Deposit money banks' assets	12.6	13.1	15.2	16.9	20.9	30.2	30.5	35.9	41.0	42.4
Deposit money banks' claims on private sector/ Deposit money banks' assets	30.5	32.8	37.1	38.8	37.4	27.8	27.8	22.5	19.2	21.9

Sources: IMF staff calculations based on Central Bank, Treasury, Ministry of Finance, and IMF data.

Note: EMBI = Emerging Markets Bond Index.

debt stock is floating interest rate instruments (in Turkish lira and foreign currency). Interest rates fluctuations, which can be quite pronounced for emerging markets, thus feed without delay into debt servicing costs. Only about one-quarter of the debt is linked to neither the exchange rate nor to current interest rates. But even that part is not immune to interest rate shocks, given that the average maturity of domestic debt is only about one year (Table 5.1).

High real interest rates and short maturities have saddled Turkey with enormous debt servicing costs. Over the past five years, the real interest rate on treasury bills was 16.5 percent on average and the spread on its eurobonds around 650 basis points. This makes for a very large interest bill—16.4 percent of GNP in 2003. Total debt service in 2003 was a staggering 49 percent of GNP or 175 percent of central government revenue.

The size of Turkey's public debt approximates the emerging market average, but this is little consolation. Public debt increased across emerging markets to reach an average of 72 percent of GNP in 2002 (IMF, 2003)—a ratio not dissimilar to that of Turkey. However, as further discussed below, there are good reasons to believe that emerging markets as a group might have overborrowed. Their debt ratios now exceed those of the advanced economies, which have debt ratios of around 65 (IMF, 2003).

Deterministic Debt Sustainability Exercise

According to this approach, public debt is deemed sustainable if the debt-to-GNP ratio remains constant or declines over time. This requirement can be expressed as a simple relationship between the primary surplus ratio (PS/GDP), the debt ratio (D/GDP), the real interest rate (r), and the rate of economic growth (g):

$$PS/GDP \geq (r - g) * D/GDP \qquad (1)$$

or equivalently

$$D/GDP \leq (PS/GDP)/(r - g). \qquad (2)$$

The critical value of the primary surplus ratio that fulfills (1) with equality is known as the "debt-stabilizing primary surplus." For smaller primary surpluses, the debt ratio explodes over time and hence is unsustainable. Equivalently, one can think of the critical value of the debt ratio that fulfills (2) with equality as a "debt threshold." For initial values of the debt ratio below the threshold, the debt position is sustainable.

Making this approach operational requires making assumptions about the real growth and interest rates that will likely prevail in the future. The primary sur-

plus is largely a policy variable that can be set by the government. The debt ratio is an observable variable, which, incidentally, depends on the exchange rate if a sizable share of the debt is denominated in, or indexed to, foreign currency.

Turkey's public finances pass the deterministic debt sustainability test. It would appear reasonable for Turkey to put the real interest rate in the vicinity of 12 percent and the real growth rate at around 5 percent. The debt ratio is currently at around 70 percent of GNP. This implies a debt-stabilizing primary surplus of 4.9 percent of GNP. As this is less than the primary surplus that the government is implementing (6.5 percent of GNP), public finances pass this debt sustainability test.

Stochastic Debt Sustainability Exercise

This approach extends the above exercise by explicitly recognizing that the underlying economic variables are stochastic. The deterministic exercise tries to simply assign the underlying economic variables their expected values. However, the future evolution of interest rates, exchange rates, and economic growth is inherently uncertain. In order to have some margin for comfort, debt should remain sustainable even under adverse circumstances. Obviously, this additional requirement raises the bar on the primary surplus, or the debt threshold, that is needed.

Exactly how resilient to adverse circumstances the debt position should be is open to debate. On the one hand, it must be recognized that the debt position of almost any country becomes unsustainable under unduly adverse circumstances. On the other, allowing for only minor deviations from the most likely scenario is risky. With this in mind, the IMF (2003) has developed some guidelines that are now routinely being applied to all member countries. The resilience of a country's debt position is tested against (i) shocks to individual variables on the order of one or two standard deviations, (ii) alternative scenarios that fix variables at their historical averages or use forecasts produced outside the IMF, and (iii) tailored tests that combine shocks to individual variables in a manner deemed relevant for the country at hand.

The sustainability of Turkey's debt position is reasonably robust to shocks, but risks remain. Adverse shocks of reasonable magnitude to individual variables can mostly be absorbed, especially if they are temporary in nature. However, unfavorable developments on several fronts at the same time could undermine sustainability. To illustrate this point, consider the following shocks relative to the quantifications in the previous section:
- If growth were permanently lower—say, 3.5 instead of 5 percent—the debt threshold would decline to 76 percent of GNP. According to formula (2), this

is still above the actual level and thus satisfies the sustainability criterion. This is even more true when the growth reduction is only transitory.

- If the real effective exchange rate depreciated by, say, 10 percent, the actual debt level would rise from 70 to 73.5 percent, as about half of Turkey's debt is effectively denominated in foreign currency. Actual debt would remain safely below the threshold of 93 percent of GNP. Debt sustainability would be maintained.
- A combination of the above growth deceleration and depreciation in conjunction with a rise of real interest rates by 1 percentage point, however, would push Turkey's public debt into unsustainability; the debt threshold would fall to 68 percent of GNP and thus exceed actual debt of 73.5 percent of GNP.

Fiscal Track Record Approach

So far, the primary surplus has been treated as if it were a policy variable, but in reality it is subject to political and technical constraints that limit the scope for fiscal adjustment. Governments often miss their fiscal targets for a variety of reasons. Budgets might be based on assumptions that involve some degree of wishful thinking, sufficient political support for fully implementing the underpinning measures might be lacking, expenditure cuts might run into legal constraints, the revenue yield from taxes has technical limits, etc.

Using an approach based on the fiscal track record yields quite low debt thresholds for emerging market economies. The IMF (2003) operationalizes this idea in two ways. The first method simply fixes the primary surplus, as well as growth and interest rates, at the average value during recent history. The debt threshold for the average emerging market economy then calculates as low as 25 percent of GNP, some two-and-a-half times less than actual levels of indebtedness. The second method allows for uncertainty in the evolution of revenue and places limits on the primary expenditure response to revenue shortfalls. The idea is to determine a safe level of debt—a level that is sustainable even if revenue falls two standard deviations short of its historical average offset by the maximum realistic primary expenditure cut (defined as the largest two-year reduction in recent history).

If the fiscal track record approach is used as a yardstick, Turkey appears to have heavily overborrowed. Applying the first method gives debt thresholds of 61, 46, and 30 percent of GNP, depending on whether three, five, or 10-year historical averages are used. According to the second method, levels of debt up to 52 percent of GNP can be considered as safe. In all cases, current levels of gross debt of around 80 percent of GNP substantially exceed thresholds.

While this approach may seem unduly pessimistic for Turkey, it is a useful reminder to remain cautious when assessing the sustainability of its debt. On the one hand, the approach is very rigid because, by construction, it forces future fiscal policy to be the same as the one pursued in the past. There is thus no room for cases where fiscal policy breaks decisively with the past—which is precisely the kind of situation one hopes is taking hold in Turkey. On the other hand, the approach is a reminder that debt levels must be low enough to also accommodate situations where fiscal targets are not always met and budgetary policies may suffer temporary setbacks at some point in the future.

Empirical Debt Sustainability

In practice, sovereign debt distress often arises at rather moderate levels of indebtedness. The history of sovereign defaults over the last three decades reveals that 55 percent of the recorded events took place when public debt was less than 60 percent of GNP. And in 35 percent of the default cases, debt was not even 40 percent of GNP (IMF, 2003). These are debt levels that advanced economies can easily support—some of them, such as Japan, Italy, and Belgium, have been living with debt ratios far in excess of 100 percent of GNP. A different yardstick seems to apply to emerging market economies and developing countries. Reinhart, Rogoff, and Savastano (2003) have coined the term "debt intolerance" for this phenomenon.

A growing empirical literature tries to identify the factors that render some countries more debt intolerant than others. Rather than analyzing country-specific debt dynamics, this literature focuses on finding those variables that explain the observed pattern of sovereign debt distress best in a statistical sense. This type of approach typically works with large sets of panel data that cover many countries and years. A plethora of potential variables is tested for its explanatory power in order to eventually arrive at a parsimonious specification that fits the data well. Identification of the key explanatory variables helps solve the puzzle of why some countries are more debt intolerant than others.

External debt relative to servicing capacity and economic volatility are consistently found to be closely associated with the emergence of sovereign debt distress. Manasse, Roubini, and Schimmelpfennig (2003) find that the likelihood of a sovereign debt crisis rises significantly with the external debt ratio, short-term external debt, and external debt service scaled by reserves. Domestic economic conditions are also significant, with unfavorable economic growth and high and volatile inflation contributing further. External developments play a role in that higher interest rates in the United States and a larger current account deficit make crises more likely. Kruger and Messmacher (2004) construct a single variable with all the information content of external debt variables: the so-called proportion of new financing needs, the ratio of external debt service and imports to the sum of exports, net external transfers, and reserves. Reinhart, Rogoff, and Savastano (2003) try to explain countries' perceived creditworthiness, as measured by the Institutional Investor Rating, and confirm the significance of the external debt ratio. In addition, a country's credit history as well as its inflation rate play an important role.

This literature holds some lessons about what can be considered a reasonably safe level of external debt in the emerging market context. Reinhart, Rogoff, and Savastano (2003) conclude that emerging markets that have not graduated to the club of countries with a very high Institutional Investor Rating, and that do not have a track record of low inflation, should not risk external debt-to-GNP ratios over 35 percent. The IMF (2003) finds external debt thresholds of 40 percent of GNP for the average nonadvanced economy, and 26 to 58 percent of GNP for low-income countries, depending on the quality of a country's policies and institutions.

Although these studies do not explicitly report results for Turkey, their general conclusions are applicable. While the studies focus on identifying the key risk factors for debt distress in emerging markets or developing countries as a group, a casual glance at the data suggests that Turkey is unlikely to score above the emerging market average in the relevant risk factors. Hence, the above stringent external debt thresholds also apply to Turkey and are currently exceeded by wide margins (Table 5.1).

Fiscal Dominance of Monetary Policy

The implications for the effectiveness of monetary policy are yet another, though related, consideration when thinking about safe levels of public indebtedness. Here the concern is that the effectiveness of the central bank's tools may be compromised once public debt reaches a certain level. The critical debt level depends on country specifics, especially the currency and maturity composition of debt, and is subject to uncertainty. As fiscal dominance is ultimately rooted in investors' concerns about public debt sustainability, one would expect that the debt thresholds derived here are not very different from those calculated in the previous sections. However, the emphasis is more on investors' perception of debt sustainability than debt sustainability per se.

Fiscal dominance implies that monetary tightening has a perverse effect on inflation, because higher interest rates raise default concerns and weaken the exchange rate. Under normal circumstances, interest rate hikes by the central bank give rise to capital inflows and an appreciation of the exchange rate. This reduces inflationary pressure together with the effects working through the standard interest and credit channels. The central bank thus has an effective tool in hand to steer inflation. A strand of literature (Giavazzi, 2003; and Blanchard, 2004) points out that this might not be the case if the government has a large outstanding debt: higher interest rates also mean higher debt servicing costs and, in the case of highly indebted countries, a higher risk of default. Capital therefore flows out of the country, the exchange rate weakens, and interest rate spreads widen. Incidentally, there are also second-round effects on debt service from the exchange rate and spreads to the extent that public debt is denominated in foreign currency or a floating rate, respectively. At any rate, the effect through this default risk channel can be powerful enough to swamp the capital flow, interest rate, and credit channels. As a result, the central bank's interest rate policy has perverse effects: a tighter interest policy causes inflation to accelerate.

The size of the public debt, conditional on its composition and other country specifics, distinguishes a monetary dominance regime from a fiscal dominance regime. At low levels of debt, default risk is not an issue and this channel simply does not apply; monetary policy operates normally. At high levels of debt, however, the default risk channel might dominate and the fiscal dominance regime applies. At what threshold of debt fiscal dominance kicks in depends on the following: (i) the higher the primary surplus, the higher the threshold, as the surplus alleviates default concerns; (ii) the higher the share of floating rate instruments or rollover rates, the lower the threshold, as these higher rates mean that monetary policy feeds more immediately into debt service costs; (iii) the higher the share of foreign and foreign currency-denominated instruments, the lower the threshold, as this share strengthens the second-round effects associated with capital outflows; and (iv) the higher the spread, the lower the threshold, as this increases debt servicing costs.

The results of some empirical studies carried out for other emerging market countries seem to indicate that fiscal dominance could also be a concern for Turkey. Blanchard (2004) and Favero and Giavazzi (2004) point to possible fiscal dominance effects in Brazil during 2002 and 2003, when markets showed concerns about the change of government. While its key variables are not identical, Turkey is generally viewed by international investors to fall into the same category as Brazil, such that their reactions to potential interest rate increases could be similar. Moreover, even if a country does not suffer from outright fiscal dominance, the conduct of its monetary policy can nonetheless be complicated by high debt.

Other Considerations

A comprehensive assessment of a country's debt position goes beyond narrow concerns about sustainability and fiscal dominance. In many ways, it is a minimum requirement that the debt position be safely bounded away from a level where shocks could make it spiral out of control or monetary policy could lose traction. But even safe debt levels might entail unduly high real interest rates or absorb a disproportionate share of bank lending.

One important additional consideration is real interest rates. The size of public debt and government borrowing requirements warrant an assessment against the depth of domestic and international capital markets available to a country. If this depth is lacking, real interest rates end up very high. This might not only imperil debt sustainability and thus further reduce the depth of the available international capital market, but it also means that the government's intertemporal consumption and investment allocation is likely far from optimal. In other words, the price for bringing government consumption and investment forward in time through borrowing might simply be too high to make it worthwhile. Turkey is indeed saddled with very high real interest rates (Table 5.1), which is tentative evidence that the country's borrowing is not commensurate with the depth of the capital markets available to it.

A second, and related, consideration is the crowding out of private sector credit from the banking system. Turkey's financial sector is relatively small to begin with. Total assets of deposit money banks amount to only about 60 percent of GNP (Table 5.1). Against this backdrop, it appears particularly problematic that claims on the government make up more than 40 percent of all bank assets. Since this leaves few resources for the private sector, it is likely holding back investment and growth.

Conclusions

How much debt is too much for Turkey? While it is not possible to be precise about a particular safe debt level, the above analysis indicates that, despite recent progress in reducing the public debt ratio, that ratio still remains too high. However, Turkey's aspirations for accession to the European Union notwithstanding, the Maastricht threshold for public debt of 60 percent of GNP is not an appropriate target, given the much more unfavorable composition of Turkey's debt compared to the average EU member country. Instead, the average public debt level of the recent EU accession countries—40 percent of GNP—might provide a sensible yardstick. That figure falls in the range of recommended thresholds found in the literature presented in this chapter. Still, this is an ambitious target for Turkey, even for the medium term.

VI Progress and Challenges in Public Debt Management

Cheng Hoon Lim

In assessing debt management operations in Turkey since 2001, this chapter focuses on how the debt structure and the institutional framework for risk management have changed since the financial crisis and what this implies for future strategies.

Turkey's financial crisis in 2001 led to a large increase in domestic debt with a structure that was highly sensitive to exchange rate and interest rates movements. The share of domestic government debt linked to or denominated in foreign currency rose sharply between 2000 and 2001 (Table 6.1), as banks sought foreign currency assets to close their short foreign exchange positions (required by tighter risk limits imposed after the crisis). The Treasury largely met the banks' demand for foreign currency assets, cognizant of the potential effect on the exchange rate if that demand were not met.

The share of floating rate notes (FRNs) in domestic central government debt rose from about 36 percent in 2000 to almost 50 percent in 2001. FRNs were issued mainly as part of the bank recapitalization effort.

Faced with a high debt burden and risky composition, investors were only prepared to hold short maturities. The average maturity of newly issued treasury bills was only 4.6 months in 2001 (Table 6.2).

Against this backdrop, Turkish authorities in 2002 implemented a comprehensive debt management program. Faced with large borrowing requirements, the authorities needed to ensure a high rollover rate and longer maturities. To this end, the Treasury formulated an action plan based on four objectives:
- Offering securities that cater to investors' needs;
- Widening the investor base;
- Improving risk management within the Treasury; and
- Deepening the liquidity of benchmark issues.

New instruments targeted the balance sheet needs of the main investors, the domestic banks, which faced tight risk constraints and had little room to take on foreign currency exposure. Thus, the size of the banks' demand for foreign currency assets was determined by their foreign currency deposits and interbank liabilities. This meant that the Treasury had to continue to issue foreign currency securities to satisfy the large demand by banks for foreign currency assets. Although there were little or no short foreign currency positions following a debt swap in 2001, banks continued to experience a shift in their liability base away from Turkish lira and into foreign currency deposits.

However, the short-term need to issue foreign currency-indexed debt created a risk for the government. If debt rollover had not been a concern, the best approach would probably have been not to accommodate the demand for foreign currency securities and instead to allow the losses that banks incurred due to their foreign currency exposure to force them to lower the interest rates they offered on their foreign currency deposits. This could have encouraged the public to move deposits into lira. However, it was uncertain at that time how quickly the demand for foreign currency deposits could be reduced, and there was a risk that some depositors would move their deposits offshore rather than switch into lira. Therefore, the Treasury decided to issue foreign currency securities to reduce market concerns about the feasibility of achieving the domestic borrowing requirement.

The Treasury also resumed the issuance of FRNs to fulfill the demand of banks for interest rate protection. The average maturity of banks' lira liabilities had shortened to about one month, thus holding even six-month treasury bills represented a significant interest rate risk for banks. FRNs offered the best prospect for lengthening maturities in lira while providing banks with the interest rate hedge that they needed.[1] In early 2002, the Treasury issued a series of two-year FRNs indexed to the three-month interest rate.

To ensure a stable and reliable source of funding, the Treasury took measures to widen its investor base. The Treasury initiated meetings with various investor groups, with an eye toward encouraging retail

---

[1]Inflation-indexed securities would have been an alternative, except that there was no demand for them. The liabilities of banks were tied to short-term interest rates, not inflation, and the correlation between nominal interest rates and inflation was too weak for inflation-indexed securities to provide an adequate hedge for bank deposits.

Table 6.1. Currency and Interest Composition of Domestic Central Government Debt

	2000	2001	2002	2003	2004
(In billions of U.S. dollars)					
Cash[1]	44.0	40.5	54.6	93.5	123.4
Fixed rate	28.9	12.3	23.0	49.2	70.7
Floating rate	13.4	7.9	10.6	20.8	27.1
Foreign currency denominated	1.8	5.0	10.1	12.1	19.8
Foreign currency indexed	...	15.3	10.9	11.4	5.8
IMF credit	...	9.6	5.9	6.1	2.8
Swap	...	5.4	4.7	5.4	3.0
Other	...	0.4	0.3	...	...
Noncash[2]	10.2	44.3	37.1	45.8	43.9
Fixed rate	1.5	...	...	...	...
Floating rate	6.0	34.4	28.6	38.8	40.1
Foreign currency denominated	2.7	8.6	7.3	5.6	2.5
Foreign currency indexed	...	1.3	1.2	1.4	1.3
Total stock[3]	54.2	84.9	91.7	139.3	167.3
(In percent of total domestic debt)					
Cash[1]	81.2	47.8	59.6	67.1	73.8
Fixed rate	53.3	14.5	25.1	35.3	42.3
Floating rate	24.7	9.3	11.6	15.0	16.2
Foreign currency denominated	3.2	5.9	11.0	8.7	11.9
Foreign currency indexed	...	18.1	11.9	8.2	3.4
IMF credit	...	11.3	6.5	4.4	1.6
Swap	...	6.4	5.1	3.8	1.8
Other	...	0.5	0.3	...	...
Noncash[2]	18.8	52.2	40.4	32.9	26.2
Fixed rate	2.8	...	...	...	...
Floating rate	11.0	40.5	31.2	27.8	24.0
Foreign currency denominated	5.0	10.1	7.9	4.1	1.5
Foreign currency indexed	...	1.5	1.3	1.0	0.8
Total stock[3]	100.0	100.0	100.0	100.0	100.0

Source: Turkish Treasury.

[1]Cash debt refers to debt issued for budget financing purposes (public and private sales).

[2]Noncash debt refers to debt issued for nonbudget financing purposes (public sales only), such as the recapitalization of state banks.

[3]For 2000, the stock of domestic debt does not include nonsecuritized debt.

and foreign participation. Investors were provided updates of recent economic developments through presentations as well as one-to-one contacts. Regular press releases were issued to provide full information to the market. To target retail investors, the authorities increased the level of interest income that was exempt from tax from TL 2 billion to TL 50 billion. By the end of 2003, retail creditors owned $23.3 billion in domestic debt instruments (Table 6.3), which amounted to 16.7 percent of the government's domestic debt stock.

At the same time, the Treasury introduced new regulations to increase transparency and accountability in debt management. As the level of public debt rose, it became more urgent to ensure that borrowing decisions were consistent with the overall macroeconomic

program and in compliance with risk and cost limits. Toward this end, the authorities introduced a new debt management law (Law No. 4749) that allowed for two important changes.

First, a debt management committee and a technical support wing (the middle office) were established within the Treasury. The middle office enhanced coordination between the domestic and foreign debt management arms of the Treasury.[2] Close cooperation between the two units was important because both

---

[2]The main task of the middle office is to formulate risk management strategies, monitor market and fiscal risk (arising from guarantees extended to public institutions), and produce quarterly debt management reports for the debt management committee, which takes the final decision on risk management policies.

Table 6.2. Maturity of Debt
(In months)

	Average Maturity of Stock	Average Maturity of New Cash Borrowing
2001 Total	38.5	18.0
Government bonds	44.5	32.9
Treasury bills	3.4	4.6
2002 Total	32.1	11.1
Government bonds	41.2	19.7
Treasury bills	4.2	6.7
2003 Total	25.1	14.7
Government bonds	28.4	20.1
Treasury bills	2.8	6.2
2004 Total	20.6	15.0
Government bonds	23.1	20.6
Treasury bills	4.5	6.2

Source: Turkish Treasury.

build-operate-transfer (BOT) projects and for external debt contracted by state-owned enterprises—was not reflected in the budget. Such lack of transparency appeared to have raised the risk premium and hence the cost of borrowing. Therefore, starting in 2003, a risk account was established to cover the contingent liabilities of the government, improving the effectiveness of cash and debt management. In addition, the ceiling that had been imposed on treasury guarantees since 1998 was extended to include BOT projects.

To help increase the liquidity of government paper, the Treasury in September 2002 reinstated the primary dealer system, which had been suspended following the financial crisis in early 2001. The main purpose was to ensure a minimum demand for government securities at primary issue and to improve secondary market liquidity by making continuous quotations of buying and selling prices on the Istanbul Stock Exchange bonds and bills market. Ten banks selected as primary dealers were required to purchase at least 5 percent of securities issued in any three-month period and at least 3 percent in any one month.

forms of borrowing contributed to meeting rollover needs and because they shared overlapping investor bases.

Second, changes were made to reflect the potential debt burden created by contingent liabilities in the budget. Before this provision of the debt law went into effect, the potential burden created by contingent liabilities—in the form of government guarantees for

Improved Debt Structure

The debt management strategy complemented sound fiscal and structural policies in 2003–04, facilitating a marked improvement in the structure of debt. The Treasury took the opportunity of an improved environment to carry out a number of debt buybacks and

Table 6.3. Outstanding Total Debt of Central Government by Lender
(In billions of U.S. dollars)

	2000	2001	2002	2003	2004
Debt by lender	94.6	123.6	148.5	202.7	235.6
Domestic debt stock	54.2	84.9	91.7	139.3	167.3
Market	...	28.8	43.3	72.9	105.2
Banks	...	...	...	24.4	...
Retail creditors	...	...	...	23.3	...
Mutual funds and legal entities	...	...	...	22.1	...
Nonresidents	...	...	...	3.0	...
Public sector	...	56.0	48.4	66.4	62.1
External debt stock	40.5	38.7	56.8	63.4	68.4
Loan	19.6	18.6	33.7	36.6	38.7
Multilateral agencies	5.6	6.4	20.6	23.5	26.2
Of which:					
IMF credit	0.5	0.5	13.9	16.7	18.4
Bilateral lenders	7.1	6.4	6.8	6.9	6.5
Commercial banks	6.8	5.8	6.3	6.1	6.0
Bond issues	20.9	20.1	23.1	26.8	29.7

Source: Turkish Treasury.

swaps to reduce the share of debt linked to foreign currency. It also started to issue two- to three-year fixed coupon bonds for the first time since the onset of the financial crisis. As a result of these operations and the enhanced debt management framework, the structure of domestic debt improved. The share of foreign currency-denominated debt in domestic debt declined to less than 18 percent by the end of 2004, compared with 32 percent in 2002 (the large foreign debt adds to this burden if total public debt is considered). In addition, the share of lira debt with a fixed rate rose from 25 percent to more than 42 percent.

The average maturity of new cash borrowing was lengthened from 11 months in 2002 to 15 months in 2004 (Table 6.2). This could not prevent a further shortening in the maturity of the overall debt stock, however, as noncash debt continued to be replaced with auctioned market debt, which typically has shorter maturities. The introduction of the primary dealer system helped enhance liquidity in the secondary market, and the daily average volume on the Istanbul Stock Exchange bonds and bills market more than tripled from its 2002 volume of only about $200 million.

Challenges Ahead for Debt Management

Despite the achievements cited above, major risks remain. Rollover requirements are still high, and despite recent improvements, Turkey's debt service remains very sensitive to movements in the exchange and interest rates. The government is still dependent on the domestic banking system to roll over maturing debt, and the Treasury's ability to lengthen maturities is therefore constrained by the liability structure of the banks. Unless the maturity of customer deposits increases—the average maturity of lira deposits stands at about three months—the demand by banks for longer-term securities may continue to be constrained.

From a debt management perspective, the authorities could take a number of measures to manage these risks. The Treasury could do more to build its cash reserves at the Central Bank to provide a larger safety cushion. Opportunistic overborrowing helps to build a useful buffer in times of need. Also, market conditions allow the Treasury to issue fixed-coupon lira debt at maturities above one year. The Treasury could use this opportunity to reduce future vulnerabilities, even if this means having to accept higher interest rates in the short term.

The authorities could also explore avenues to further diversify the investor base by:

- Increasing demand from insurance and pension funds. In many countries, such institutions provide a large part of the demand for longer-term government securities. In Turkey, these institutions are not yet fully developed. Their development could also raise demand for inflation-indexed securities.[3]
- Investigating the potential to increase corporate demand for government securities, a largely untapped source that could be useful particularly if companies have in-house pension plans for employees.
- Promoting treasury bills through the state banks' extensive retail network.
- Reviewing the tax treatment of various debt instruments and removing any distortions or impediments.
- Encouraging foreign investors to hold domestic debt by providing good quality data and frequent updates of changes in government strategies. The Treasury could consider setting up an independent investor relations office as a permanent structure to provide a focal point of contact between the authorities and investors.

---

[3]These bonds have a number of benefits. In particular, they can (i) strengthen the credibility and commitment of authorities to monetary policy, and provide useful information to policymakers about inflation expectations; (ii) reduce rollover risk and contribute to the development of long-term benchmarks; and (iii) allow authorities to issue external debt denominated in local currency, thus protecting the sovereign from the risk of currency depreciation.

VII Lessons from an Empirical Model of Fiscal Policy in Emerging Markets

Xavier Debrun

The degree and sustainability of "fiscal effort" in Turkey can be measured using a simple empirical model of fiscal policy behavior that integrates the role played by economic, political, and fiscal institutional factors.[1] The model provides estimates of feasible primary surplus targets that reflect the state of the economy, the stock of public debt, the quality of economic governance, past adjustment efforts, and the institutional capacity to generate surpluses.

The analysis suggests that the targeted primary surplus of 6.5 percent of GNP in 2004 could be achieved with the same degree of effort as in 2003. However, over the medium run, fiscal reforms (whose positive effect on the surplus-generating capacity is estimated to be between 1.5 and 2.5 percent of GNP) seem critical to sustain high primary surpluses. The analysis also indicates that greater political stability and further improvements in economic governance would lower the necessary level of primary surpluses, as borrowing costs would fall in response to stronger policy credibility. Broad-based structural reforms thus appear as an important avenue to progressively alleviate the burden of high primary surpluses while maintaining ambitious debt reduction goals.

Debt Sustainability and the Primary Surplus

From an accounting perspective, the necessary primary balance consistent with debt sustainability depends on growth, interest rates, and the stock of liabilities. In normal circumstances, if the objective of the medium-term fiscal strategy is to reduce the debt-to-GDP ratio, b, the government will have to target a primary surplus $\bar{p}_t$ such that $\bar{p}_t > b_t(r - g)$, where r is the real interest rate and g

the real growth rate. The more ambitious the debt reduction objective, the higher the primary surplus target.

However, in practice, the appropriate primary surplus target goes beyond accounting identities and needs to reflect what the authorities can credibly achieve. For example, a key factor is the strength of fiscal institutions, notably in terms of their capacity to raise revenue and control expenditure. Another factor affecting the credibility of fiscal targets is the success of previous fiscal adjustment episodes. A situation in which repeated fiscal slippages have put at risk the perception of a government's ability to honor its commitment would be particularly challenging. On the one hand, keeping debt dynamics under control may require historically high primary surplus targets. On the other, excessively high targets may be self-defeating, as creditors price in a high likelihood of failure of the adjustment strategy. Hence, when debt sustainability is at risk, it is essential to anchor the inevitably high primary surplus targets in a coherent reform strategy that lifts the capacity to sustain these surpluses in the short run while reducing the need to maintain them for too long.

The Empirical Model

The cross-country empirical model used in this chapter follows Bohn (1998), but is extended to quantify the effect of institutions on fiscal behavior. The model accounts for cross-country heterogeneity with country fixed effects and nonlinearities in the relationship between the dependent variable and explanatory variables. It is written as:

$$p_{i,t} = \alpha_i + \rho b_{i,t-1} + \beta D_i \left(b_{i,t-1} - b^* \right) + \gamma Z_{i,t} + \delta Z_{i,t} b_{i,t-1}$$
$$+ \sum_{j=1}^{J} \beta_j X_{j,i,t} + \sum_{j=1}^{J} \eta_j Z_{i,t} X_{j,i,t} + \varepsilon_{i,t} \qquad (1)$$

where $p_{i,t}$ is the primary balance in country i at time t; $b_{i,t-1}$ is the public debt in country i at the end of period $t - 1$; α_i is a country-specific intercept (fixed effect); $\varepsilon_{i,t}$ is an error term; Z denotes the institutional quality indicator; and X_j's are cyclical variables explaining changes in the primary balance unrelated to

---
[1]The model draws on and extends work published in the September 2003 edition of the International Monetary Fund's *World Economic Outlook*. The current variant of the model was reestimated using the most recent fiscal data for Turkey.

Table 7.1. Panel Estimates of the Fiscal Policy Equation

(Dependent variable: primary balance in percentage of GDP)

Variable	Coefficient	t-Statistics	p-Value
Output gap	−0.081	−1.114	0.260
Public debt (t−1)	0.128	8.911	0.000
Spline (50 percent)	−0.129	−8.254	0.000
Institutional quality	−0.543	−4.765	0.000
Interactions			
Debt and institutions	0.002	1.005	0.316
Output gap and			
institutions	0.054	3.242	0.001
Inflation	0.001	5.728	0.000
Oil prices	0.068	2.434	0.016
Nonoil commodities prices	0.067	2.171	0.031
Default-restructuring dummy	0.477	2.683	0.008
Weighted R-squared		0.662	
Unweighted R-squared		0.504	
Number of observations		244	

Note: Feasible generalized least square estimates with robust standard errors. Country fixed effects not reported.

the long-run solvency requirement.[2] Finally, equation (1) also allows for a "spline" parameter that captures a possible break in the relationship between debt and the primary surplus at a debt level b^*; D_i is a dummy variable equal to 1 when $b_{i,t-1} > b^*$ and to zero otherwise.

Key Results

The model is estimated using a panel of 23 emerging market economies—including Turkey—over the period from 1990–2002.[3] Fiscal policy is described by the primary balance of the general government (or the closest available entity). The quality of economic governance is captured by an indicator averaging indices of government stability, bureaucratic quality, and perceived corruption from the International Country Risk Guide (Political Risk Services Group, 2003). X_j's are proxied by the output gap and inflation (for commodity exporters, deviations of oil and nonoil commodity prices from their Hodrick-Prescott [HP] trend are also included).

The estimated coefficients of equation (1) confirm the significant role of institutional variables (Table 7.1). However, the overall effect on the primary surplus is ambiguous, as the estimates reveal the following three channels through which institutional factors work:

- Better institutions are associated with lower surpluses, suggesting a reduced need to generate large primary surpluses, presumably because the authorities' commitment to honor obligations is more credible. Hence, good institutions—as reflected by political stability, low levels of corruption, and a high-quality bureaucracy—would tend to allow countries to borrow at a lower cost and with longer maturities, thereby reducing the primary surplus consistent with solvency at any given level of debt.
- Stronger institutions are associated with a greater countercyclicality of fiscal policy, which indicates better control of expenditures during booms, when revenue windfalls and easier financial conditions make spending increases difficult to resist. Procyclical fiscal policies are frequently observed in emerging market economies (see Talvi and Végh, 2000; and Tornell and Lane, 1999), and can easily lead to a deficit bias if procyclical loosening is less than offset by procyclical tightening. This is generally the case. Good institutions limit that risk and contribute to healthier primary balances.
- Better institutions are associated with a greater concern for solvency, as the primary surplus responds more strongly to stabilize the public debt ratio. However, this result is imprecisely estimated and should therefore be treated with caution.

The country fixed effects provide additional information on surplus-generating capacity. Although they capture any country-specific feature systematically affecting fiscal performance, they also encapsulate key features of the fiscal regime relevant for surplus-generating potential, such as weak expenditure control and low revenue-raising capacity. Figure 7.1 depicts a positive relationship between the government revenue-

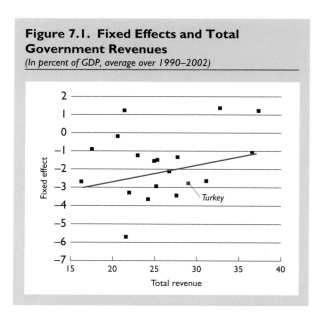

Figure 7.1. Fixed Effects and Total Government Revenues

(In percent of GDP, average over 1990–2002)

---

[2]See Favero (2002), Gali and Perotti (2003), and Fatás and Mihov (2003) for detailed discussions of the issues related to the specification for fiscal policy equations.

[3]The total sample contains 34 countries. See IMF (2003) for details.

Figure 7.2. Revenue Ratios and Effective Tax Rates in Selected Emerging Market Economies

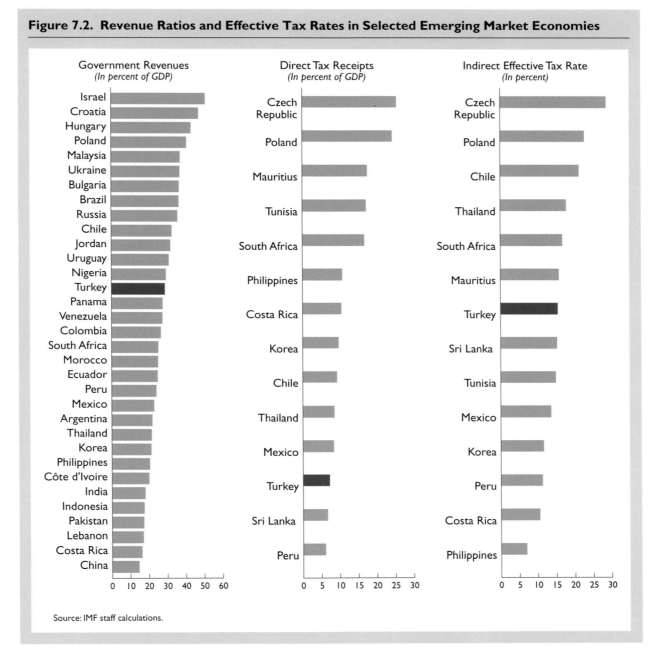

Source: IMF staff calculations.

to-GNP ratio and the estimated fixed effects.[4] The relatively low revenue-to-GNP ratios characteristic of many emerging market economies partly explain why, on average and irrespective of the role of other factors (such as institutions), these economies find it difficult to generate the high primary surpluses required to sta-bilize high levels of public debt (see Figure 7.2). As Table 7.1 confirms, the debt-stabilizing response of the primary surplus weakens considerably (and in fact disappears) once public debt exceeds 50 percent of GNP.[5]

---

[4]Figure 7.1 excludes the transition economies, namely Poland, Hungary, Ukraine, and Russia, which are more in line with advanced economies than typical emerging market economies.

[5]The 50 percent threshold maximizes the model's goodness of fit. As shown in IMF (2003), such a break in the debt-stabilizing response of fiscal policy sharply contrasts with the behavior of fiscal authorities in advanced economies, which tends to raise the debt-stabilizing response of the primary surplus once the public debt ratio exceeds 80 percent of GNP.

The Case of Turkey

For Turkey, the model is used to generate predicted values for the primary surplus. These can then be compared to actual levels, and a measure of "fiscal effort" can be derived as the difference between actual and predicted primary surpluses (that is, the residuals of the regression). Table 7.2 shows significant adjustment efforts starting in 2000 and continuing through 2004, when the effort needed to reach the 6.5 percent target is estimated to remain high, at 4.2 percent of GNP. By definition, positive "residuals" cannot be observed for long unless a structural break in fiscal behavior occurs. In practice, this means that sustaining the high primary surpluses consistent with a rapid reduction in the debt-to-GNP ratio makes structural reforms an essential part of the consolidation strategy.

Turkey's low country fixed effect in relation to revenues suggests that the surplus-generating potential can be improved by enhancing expenditure management. In Figure 7.1, the expected increase can be measured by the vertical distance separating Turkey from the regression line, which is 1.3 percentage points of GNP. There is thus merit in paying particular attention to expenditure management in the fiscal reform plan. In that respect, it is worth noting that the low country fixed effect is reflected one-for-one in the average fiscal effort reported in Table 7.2. Hence, fiscal reforms resulting in a greater fixed effect would reduce the measured effort, bringing the current consolidation strategy in line with "normal," and therefore more easily sustained, fiscal behavior.

On the revenue side, there also seems to be potential for improvement. In comparison with other emerging market economies, Turkey's total revenue ratio is not high. Besides, the direct tax-to-GNP ratio is strikingly low (Figure 7.2), whereas the indirect effective tax rate is above average for emerging market economies. This lends support to the view that tax administration and tax policy reform, along with a rebalancing in the composition of revenues, could prove fruitful.

The results bring to the fore the issue of the highest feasible primary surplus given Turkey's economic situation and institutions. Table 7.2 considers various pos-

Table 7.2. Alternative Measures of Feasible Primary Surpluses
(Nonfinancial public sector, in percent of GDP)

	1991	1992	1993	1994	1995	1996	1997	1998	1999	2000	2001	2002	2003	2004	Average 1993–2003[3]
Actual primary balance:[1] (a)	n.a.	n.a.	−5.6	−0.2	2.7	−1.2	−2.1	0.5	−2.0	3.0	5.5	4.2	6.2	6.5	1.0
Predicted primary balance: (b)	−0.8	−1.4	0.0	−1.5	0.4	−0.1	0.7	1.6	−0.2	1.8	0.4	1.7	2.0	2.3	0.6
Relative adjustment effort:[2] (c) = (a)−(b)	n.a.	n.a.	−5.6	1.3	2.3	−1.1	−2.8	−1.1	−1.8	1.2	**5.1**	2.4	4.2	4.2	2.7
Measures of feasible surplus:															
(b) + maximum effort over 1993–2003	4.2	3.6	5.1	3.6	5.5	4.9	5.7	6.6	4.9	6.9	5.5	6.8	7.1	7.3	5.7
(b) + average positive effort 1993–2003	1.9	1.3	2.7	1.3	3.2	2.6	3.4	4.3	2.6	4.5	3.2	4.5	4.7	5.0	3.4
(b) with "ambitious" fiscal reforms[4]	1.9	1.3	2.8	1.3	3.2	2.6	3.4	4.3	2.6	4.6	3.2	4.5	4.8	5.0	3.4
(b) + average positive effort 1993–2003, and "ambitious" fiscal reforms	4.7	4.1	5.5	4.1	5.9	5.4	6.2	7.1	5.3	7.3	6.0	7.3	7.5	7.8	6.1
(b) + average positive effort 1993–2003, and fiscal reforms[5]	3.2	2.7	4.1	2.6	4.5	3.9	4.8	5.6	3.9	5.9	4.5	5.8	6.1	6.3	4.7
Memo items: Total revenue	22.8	24.1	25.3	25.6	23.7	24.6	27.1	29.6	32.1	39.4	38.8	34.3	34.8	...	30.5
Average fixed effect in primary surplus equation							−1.8								
Turkey fixed effect in primary surplus equation							−2.8								
Expected Turkey fixed effect on the basis of revenues							−1.3								

[1]Targeted surplus for 2004 as in the "program baseline" of the fiscal strategy note.
[2]The average is based only on positive efforts.
[3]The average fiscal effort is calculated based on the positive numbers only.
[4]The potential effect of "ambitious" fiscal reforms on the surplus-generating capacity is estimated as (minus) the country's fixed effect in the primary surplus model.
[5]The primary surplus effect of fiscal reforms is estimated as the difference between the country fixed effect and the predicted fixed effect on the basis of revenues (see Figure 7.2).

sibilities, based on the continuation of past consolidation efforts (that is, ignoring negative values of the effort variable in the sample) and on the plausible benefits of fiscal reforms. Depending on the methodology used, the feasible range is estimated to be between 3.5 percent and just over 6 percent of GNP, on average. Clearly, more ambitious reforms and greater effort could, of course, deliver higher surpluses. However, structural improvements in expenditure control and revenue-raising capacity would likely be needed to avoid adjustment fatigue, given the degree of recent fiscal effort.

Further insights into risks to the sustainability of fiscal efforts can be gained from simple descriptive statistics of fiscal adjustments undertaken in the sample. An interesting first question is how persistent have fiscal adjustments been. Persistent fiscal adjustment is defined here by two criteria: (i) a large initial adjustment (that is, an initial increase of 1 percent of GNP in the primary balance, which turns out to be the threshold for the 75th percentile of all adjustments in the sample); and (ii) an average primary balance over the three

subsequent years that is at least 1.5 percent higher than at the end of the initial year.

Although 60 cases satisfy the large-initial-adjustment criterion, only 10 of them pass the persistence criterion. For these persistent adjustment cases, Figure 7.3 shows in the top panel the typical path of primary balance three years before and up to five years after the initial adjustment year. The median adjustment over six years (from $t-1$ to $t+5$) turns out to be quite large (on the order of 6 percentage points of GNP). The bottom panel of Figure 7.3 compares the adjustment path with the median, and indicates that the adjustment path in Turkey is somewhat higher than the median path of persistent adjustments, especially at the end of the period (2003–04).

But how does Turkey's adjustment compare against all other attempts (failed as well as successful) in the sample? Figure 7.4 shows the probability distribution

Figure 7.3. Successful Fiscal Adjustments in Emerging Market Economies

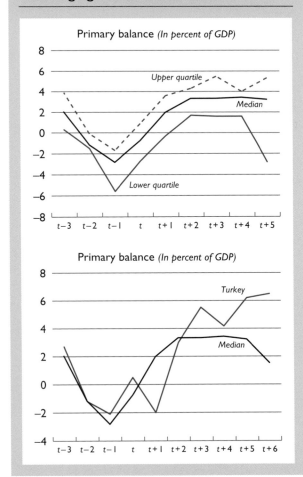

Figure 7.4. Probability Distribution of Fiscal Adjustment in Emerging Market Economies

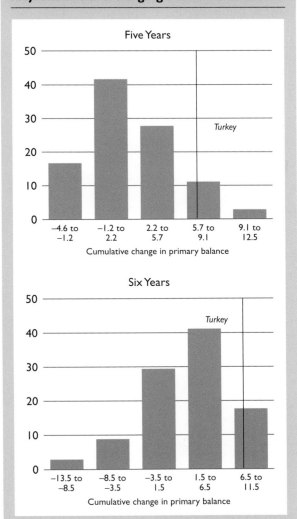

of cumulative fiscal adjustment after four, five, and six years. Although not without precedent, Turkey's fiscal adjustment would be unusually successful if maintained, when compared to all other cases of intensive adjustment.

Conclusions

The empirical evidence presented in this chapter indicates that, by any measure, the recent fiscal adjustment in Turkey has been remarkable in size and longevity, at least when compared to a sample of 34 emerging market economies over the period from 1990–2002. If maintained, it would easily qualify as one of the few successful (persistent) adjustment episodes in that sample.

The challenge now is to sustain Turkey's strong performance. More specifically, the challenge is to reduce the debt ratio at least to below 50 percent, the threshold identified by the econometric analysis in this chapter as an upper limit to what a typical emerging market economy can sustain without endangering long-run sustainability. The empirical evidence points to a risk of adjustment fatigue, as large fiscal efforts can hardly be continued without a permanent change in fiscal behavior. It therefore appears critical to anchor the medium-term fiscal consolidation strategy in a broad structural reform package that would at the same time boost the surplus-generating potential of the country and progressively reduce the need for exceptionally high surpluses. From that perspective, the analysis points to expenditure and tax policy reforms as two clear areas of priority.

VIII Sustainability of the Fiscal Adjustment

Ernesto Ramirez Rigo

This chapter examines the composition of Turkey's numerous fiscal adjustments over the last decade in the context of academic literature that analyzes the cross-country experience of what constitutes a successful fiscal adjustment. The comparison shows that the composition of Turkey's most recent fiscal adjustment may need to be rebalanced if it is to be sustained for a prolonged period.

Emerging market countries often have to undertake sustained fiscal consolidation in quite difficult circumstances. In contrast with industrial countries, where adjustments are usually driven by the needs of demand management, emerging market countries often have to adjust because of debt sustainability concerns. As a result, the fiscal consolidation effort generally needs to be maintained for a longer time to achieve debt sustainability.

The composition of fiscal adjustment is critical to the success of longer-term fiscal consolidation. Short-term improvements in fiscal balance can be achieved by a wide variety of policy actions on revenues or expenditures. But when the objective is to maintain the improvement over a longer period of time, the composition of the adjustment can increase the chances of sustaining the consolidation. Alesina and Perotti (1996) studied the composition of fiscal adjustments in countries in the Organization for Economic Cooperation and Development (OECD) from the early 1960s to the mid-1990s to explain the sustainability of the adjustments.[1] They found that countries with the most durable fiscal improvements were those that had placed the most effort toward reducing expenditures (especially sensitive items such as wages and transfers). Adjustments in countries that had implemented revenue increases and capital expenditure cuts tended to be shorter lived.

For countries with debt sustainability problems, the benefits are greatest if the fiscal effort is seen as permanent. When debt is on a potentially unsustainable path, this adds to the urgency of adjusting. The costs of failure are increased, but at the same time these countries can benefit the most from any fall in real interest rates that results from consolidation. Increasing revenues through tax hikes does not seem to have the same positive effects as expenditure cuts because tax increases can be quite easily reversed. Tax increases can also have adverse effects on the economy and weaken the resolve to maintain the adjustment. Also, expenditure cuts that fall on investment are less likely to be seen as permanent and may affect long-term economic prospects.

However, some caution is needed in applying results from the industrial country experience to the problems of emerging market economies. Industrial countries usually have large welfare states, high levels of public employment, and high tax rates. Nonindustrial countries tend to have smaller welfare states and generally lower tax rates. Thus, it is possible that what determines the success in an industrial economy may not apply to emerging markets. For example, a recent study by Gupta and others (2002) found that revenue-increasing measures could play a useful role in middle-income countries. Even so, emerging countries that reduce the wage bill and other current spending were more likely to be successful in sustaining their consolidations.

Fiscal Adjustments

Turkey has undertaken a number of large fiscal adjustments over the past decade, with varying degrees of success. In 1993, Turkey had a general government fiscal primary deficit of more than 5 percent of GNP (Table 8.1). Over 1994–95, the government undertook an adjustment of 8.3 percent of GNP, turning the 1993 deficit into a surplus of 2.7 percent of GNP by 1995. However, this adjustment was short lived, and the fiscal primary balance fell into deficit again in 1996–97. In 1998, there was another attempt at fiscal adjustment, but this also unraveled soon afterwards. The most recent adjustment came in 2000, and this has so far been successful in improving the primary balance by more than

---

[1]They defined a fiscal adjustment in terms of a negative fiscal impulse of 1.5 percent of GDP or more and defined an adjustment as successful when, three years after the adjustment, the debt-to-GDP ratio was 5 percentage points lower.

Table 8.1. Summary of Primary Surpluses
(In percent of GNP)

	1993	1994	1995	1996	1997	1998	1999	2000	2001	2002	2003
Consolidated budget	−0.9	3.6	3.2	1.6	−0.2	4.1	1.4	5.0	5.0	2.6	4.9
Rest of public sector	−4.7	−3.8	−0.5	−2.8	−1.9	−3.6	−3.4	−2.0	0.5	1.5	1.3
Primary surplus	**−5.6**	**−0.2**	**2.7**	**−1.2**	**−2.1**	**0.5**	**−2.0**	**3.0**	**5.5**	**4.2**	**6.2**
Change in primary surplus		**5.4**	**2.9**	**−3.9**	**−0.9**	**2.6**	**−2.5**	**5.0**	**2.5**	**−1.3**	**2.0**
Change from consolidated budget	4.5	−0.4	−1.7	−1.7	4.3	−2.7	3.6	0.0	−2.3	2.3	
Change from rest of public sector	0.9	3.3	−2.2	0.8	−1.7	0.2	1.3	2.6	1.0	−0.3	
Memorandum items											
GNP (real growth rate)	8.4	−5.0	6.9	6.9	7.6	3.1	−4.7	7.4	−7.5	7.9	5.8
Net debt to GNP	35.1	44.7	41.3	46.5	42.9	43.7	61.0	58.3	93.9	79.2	70.9

Source: Ministry of Finance and IMF estimates.

8 percent of GNP. Given Turkey's track record, however, it may be instructive to reexamine the earlier failed adjustments in order to identify their strengths and weaknesses, and to use these findings to determine how to improve the chances of success of the current adjustment.

Defining a "Successful" Adjustment Episode

As a preliminary step, what constitutes a "successful" fiscal adjustment needs to be defined. For many countries, fiscal adjustment can best be defined in terms of changes in the overall balance. However, in Turkey's case, any definition should also take into account potential problems from debt composition. The large share of foreign currency debt and its short maturity makes the overall balance very volatile. Since the interest bill is largely outside the direct control of policymakers, changes in the overall balance may not be representative of policy efforts, and the primary balance should be preferred instead. A key question then is the coverage of the primary surplus. Large fiscal operations outside the central government budget, including numerous state enterprises with quasi-fiscal operations, would call for a definition that covers the general government. However, it is difficult to obtain reliable information on off-budget operations and state-owned enterprises. Thus, while the adjustment is defined here in terms of the general government primary surplus, the composition of the adjustment can only be examined at the consolidated budget level.

Thus, fiscal adjustment episodes are defined here as when the change in the general government primary surplus was 2.5 percent of GNP in a year or 5 percent of GNP in two consecutive years. Such an adjustment

is considered successful when the primary surplus does not fall by more than 2 percent of GNP two years after the adjustment.

In identifying episodes of fiscal adjustment, the impact of the business cycle should also be considered. Year-to-year changes in the primary surplus may be driven not only by policy effort, but also by changes in economic conditions that affect the primary balance via the automatic stabilizers. Thus, following Alesina and Perotti (1996), this chapter considers as episodes of fiscal adjustment only those times when there is a negative fiscal impulse (Figure 8.1).

Measurement of the composition of the adjustment should also be corrected for the cycle. This is approached here in two different ways. The first assumes that the elasticities of revenues and expenditures to GNP are unity. This allows for looking at the changes in the primary surplus as a ratio to GNP as fully driven by discretionary policy. The problem with this approach is that revenues may have larger elasticities—as a result, for example, of the progressive personal income tax system. Also, high inflation can have a significant impact on expenditures and revenues from year to year. As a result of these concerns, the second method estimates cyclically-neutral expenditures and revenues for the period. The difference between the estimated revenues and expenditures and the actual budget outcomes is then regarded as the policy effort.[2]

_____

[2]We have used the OECD formulation for fiscal impulse and for the estimate of cyclical effects on revenues and neutral expenditures: $FI = [(Gt - Tt) - (Gt - 1 * (1 + \tilde{y}t) - Tt - 1 * (1 + \alpha yt))]/Yt$, where FI is the fiscal impulse; G is primary expenditure; T is government revenues; y is actual nominal growth rate of GNP; Y is actual nominal GNP; $\tilde{y}$ is the estimated potential real GNP growth rate plus the actual GNP deflator; and α is revenue elasticity to GNP.

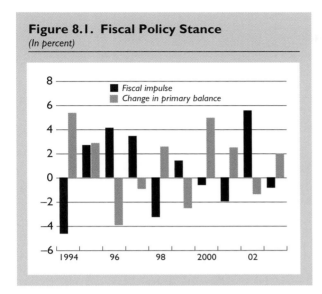

Figure 8.1. Fiscal Policy Stance
(In percent)

Using this definition, three significant episodes of fiscal adjustment in Turkey have been identified over the past 10 years. The first was in 1994–95, when the primary surplus increased by 8.3 percent of GNP; the second in 1998, with an adjustment of 2.6 percent of GNP; and the third in 2000–01, when the primary surplus increased by 7.5 percent of GNP. The first and last episodes are large adjustments by any standard. In addition, both were multiyear adjustments, and in both cases the consolidated budget and the rest of the public sector contributed to the effort almost in an equal manner (Table 8.1).

Using another definition explained earlier, only the 2000–01 adjustment can be considered successful. The 1994–95 adjustment failed to be sustained, since in the two years that followed more than half of it unraveled. Likewise, the 1998 adjustment was fully unraveled in 1999. On the other hand, in the case of the 2000–01 adjustment, the primary surplus did not fall by more than 2 percent of GNP two years afterwards—in fact, it has continued to increase.

However, it is paradoxical that the two adjustments that failed apparently had compositions that should have made them sustainable (Table 8.2). The adjustment in 1994–95 was mostly based on expenditure reduction, although revenue mobilization also played a small role. In 1994, 65 percent of the improvement in the primary surplus of the central government was due to expenditure reduction, with composition such that it would have been expected to result in a lasting adjustment. Noninterest current spending was reduced significantly, and cuts in the wage bill represented more than one-third of the total adjustment. In 1998, the composition of the adjustment was more balanced between revenues and expenditures. However, like in

1994–95, cuts in noninterest current spending were a key element of the adjustment.

In contrast, the 2000–01 adjustment was driven mainly by revenue increases. In 2000, 70 percent of the improvement in the primary surplus came from revenue increases, especially indirect taxes (value-added tax rates were raised 2 percentage points). For the two year period of 2000–01, the cumulative adjustment was entirely due to revenue increases. Primary expenditures were allowed to grow, particularly the government wage bill and the Social Security deficits. This composition would not seem to bode well for a lasting adjustment, yet it was sustained for at least two years.

As a cross-check, the raw figures for fiscal adjustment were reestimated to include the effects of the business cycle (Table 8.3). To do this, we have estimated cyclically neutral revenues and expenditures, and compared these with the actual budget outcomes. The growth rate of potential real GNP was estimated using a Hodrick-Prescott filter and used to forecast revenues and expenditures. Revenues were assumed to grow with actual nominal GNP, estimating the elasticity by using the average buoyancy of revenues with respect to GNP growth, and expenditures to grow with potential GNP. The difference between these estimated cyclically neutral revenues and expenditures and the actual outcomes can be used as a measure of policy effort.

Correcting for the business cycle changes the composition of adjustment somewhat, but the basic conclusions are unchanged.[3] The revised estimates for 1994–95 suggest that the entire adjustment came from expenditure reduction, and that taxes were even allowed to decline. In 1998, the fiscal adjustment was still shared between expenditures and revenues, although the cyclically-adjusted estimates point to an even larger reduction of expenditures. When the cyclical adjustment is made, the results for 2000–01 suggest that the effort is more balanced between revenues and expenditures than the raw data suggest, with almost 40 percent of the adjustment coming from reductions in primary expenditure. Still, the overall picture is the same: the first two episodes were based mainly on expenditure adjustment, while the last one relied much more on revenue measures.

However, other factors aside from the composition of adjustment may have played a key role in the sustainability of these episodes of fiscal consolidation. Perhaps the more important factor behind the lack of success in the first two adjustments was political. Both adjustments took place under weak coalition governments. The unraveling of these governments and the ensuing

---

[3]The results from these estimates are sensitive to changes in the assumptions. For example, increasing the potential growth rate and the revenue elasticity would tilt the estimated composition of adjustment toward expenditure reduction.

Table 8.2. Central Government Operations and Composition of Adjustment
(In percent of GNP)

	1994	1995	1996	1997	1998	1999	2000	2001	2002	2003
Revenue	18.3	17.0	17.3	18.6	20.7	22.1	24.6	25.7	23.9	25.6
Tax revenue	14.3	13.0	14.3	15.3	16.2	17.4	19.8	20.9	19.7	21.4
Direct	5.5	5.3	5.6	6.2	7.6	7.7	8.0	8.4	6.5	6.9
Indirect	8.8	7.7	8.7	9.1	8.6	9.7	11.8	12.4	13.2	14.5
Nontax revenue	4.0	4.0	3.0	3.3	4.5	4.6	4.8	4.9	4.2	4.1
Primary expenditure	14.7	13.8	15.7	18.8	16.6	20.7	19.6	20.7	21.3	20.6
Noninterest current spending	12.8	12.5	14.0	16.6	14.8	18.7	17.6	18.4	18.7	18.6
Personnel	7.0	6.4	6.5	7.1	7.2	8.8	7.9	8.6	8.4	8.5
Investment	2.0	1.3	1.7	2.2	1.9	2.0	2.0	2.4	2.5	2.0
Primary surplus (−deficit)	**3.6**	**3.2**	**1.6**	**−0.2**	**4.1**	**1.4**	**5.0**	**5.0**	**2.6**	**4.9**
Change in surplus	**4.5**	**−0.4**	**−1.7**	**−1.7**	**4.3**	**−2.7**	**3.6**	**0.0**	**−2.3**	**2.3**
Composition of adjustment Change in percent of GNP										
Revenue	**1.6**	**−1.3**	0.3	1.3	**2.1**	1.3	**2.6**	1.1	−1.8	1.7
Tax revenue	**2.1**	**−1.3**	1.3	1.0	**0.9**	1.2	**2.4**	1.1	−1.1	1.7
Direct	**−0.1**	**−0.2**	0.3	0.6	**1.4**	0.1	**0.3**	0.5	−1.9	0.4
Indirect	**2.2**	**−1.1**	1.0	0.4	**−0.4**	1.1	**2.1**	0.6	0.7	1.3
Nontax revenue	**−0.6**	**0.0**	−1.0	0.3	**1.2**	0.1	**0.2**	0.0	−0.7	0.0
Primary expenditure	**−2.9**	**−0.9**	1.9	3.0	**−2.2**	4.1	**−1.1**	1.1	0.5	−0.6
Noninterest current spending	**−2.0**	**−0.3**	1.5	2.6	**−1.9**	4.0	**−1.1**	0.7	0.4	−0.1
Personnel	**−1.5**	**−0.6**	0.1	0.5	**0.2**	1.6	**−0.9**	0.7	−0.2	0.1
Investment	**−0.9**	**−0.7**	0.4	0.5	**−0.3**	0.1	**0.0**	0.4	0.2	−0.5
Memorandum item Cumulative improvement from revenues	34.7	6.4			49.4		70.2	100.0		72.1
Cumulative improvement from expenditures	65.3	93.6			50.6		29.8	0.0		27.9
Cumulative improvement from wage bill	32.7	50.7			−4.2		24.3	5.8		−3.2

Source: Ministry of Finance Public Accounts Bulletins.

elections tended to result in an unwinding of the fiscal consolidation. The current, more successful adjustment was also initiated by a coalition government, and it too showed signs of unraveling in the run-up to elections in 2002. The election of a strong single-party government may have been key to ensuring the continuation of the consolidation. Another key factor may have been the growing concern over debt sustainability. In 1994 and 1998, debt sustainability concerns were not yet at a critical stage, so there was seemingly less cost to slippage. But during the 2000–01 crisis, debt sustainability emerged as the main concern. The cost of failure was so great that unsuccessful fiscal consolidation could not be contemplated.

In addition, the analysis presented earlier is very aggregate and does not capture well the quality of individual expenditure measures. Although the first two fiscal adjustments relied on expenditure reduction, the measures may have been of poor quality and therefore unsustainable. Although the reduction in the wage bill

in 1994–95 was impressive, it did not deal with the underlying problem of growing public sector employment. The wage bill as a share of GNP in 1995 was still almost 0.5 percent higher than in 1989, and the adjustment of 1994–95 seemed to have been due more to inflation surprises than design, and was therefore difficult to sustain over time. Finally, despite measures to curtail primary expenditures in 1994–95 and 1998, the Social Security deficit was allowed to continue to grow, rising from 0.5 percent of GNP in 1993 to 2.6 percent of GNP in 1998.

Implementation of structural reforms may also help support the latest adjustment. The institutional framework for fiscal policy has been strengthened. Together with a significant reduction in off-budget operations, this might help maintain fiscal control. This was missing in earlier episodes. There also has been a significant effort to curtail quasi-fiscal operations in state enterprises. Measuring the composition of adjustment at the budget level misses these developments in the rest of the

Table 8.3. Estimate of Composition of Adjustment
(In percent of GNP)

	1994	1995	1996	1997	1998	1999	2000	2001	2002	2003
Revenues (actual)	18	17	17	19	21	22	25	26	24	26
Primary expenditures (actual)	15	14	16	19	17	21	20	21	21	21
Projected performance										
Revenue	**17.9**	**19.6**	**18.2**	**18.5**	**19.8**	**21.7**	**23.2**	**25.6**	**27.0**	**24.7**
Tax revenue	13.1	15.5	14.0	15.4	16.4	17.1	18.5	20.7	22.1	20.5
Direct	5.8	5.7	5.5	5.8	6.4	7.8	7.9	8.1	8.6	6.6
Indirect	7.3	9.8	8.6	9.7	10.0	9.3	10.6	12.7	13.5	13.9
Nontax revenue	4.8	4.2	4.2	3.2	3.5	4.7	4.8	5.0	5.0	4.3
Primary expenditure	**19.0**	**13.7**	**12.5**	**15.2**	**19.0**	**18.9**	**18.9**	**22.6**	**18.8**	**20.6**
Estimated policy effort (actual-projected)										
Revenue	**0.4**	**−2.6**	**−0.8**	**0.1**	**0.9**	**0.4**	**1.4**	**0.1**	**−3.1**	**0.9**
Tax revenue	1.2	−2.5	0.3	−0.1	−0.2	0.4	1.3	0.1	−2.3	1.0
Direct	−0.3	−0.4	0.1	0.4	1.2	−0.1	0.1	0.3	−2.1	0.3
Indirect	1.5	−2.1	0.1	−0.6	−1.4	0.5	1.2	−0.2	−0.3	0.6
Nontax revenue	−0.8	−0.2	−1.2	0.1	1.0	0.0	0.0	−0.1	−0.9	−0.1
Primary expenditure	**−4.2**	**0.1**	**3.3**	**3.6**	**−2.4**	**1.8**	**0.8**	**−1.9**	**2.5**	**0.0**
Memorandum										
Cumulative improvement from revenues	9.2	−52.8								
Cumulative improvement from expenditures	94.8	100.6								
Fiscal impulse	−4.7	2.7	4.1	3.4	−3.3	1.4	−0.6	−2.0	5.6	−0.9

Source: IMF staff estimates.

public sector. For example, in 2000–01 a substantial effort went into eliminating implicit subsidies and redundant employment in state economic enterprises.

Conclusions

Turkey's experience does not appear to sit well with the main findings in the literature on successful fiscal adjustment. Earlier episodes of large fiscal adjustment had a composition that should have increased the probability of success, yet they unraveled quickly. Conversely, the current adjustment, with its emphasis on revenue measures, would be expected to be short lived, yet it has been sustained for more than two years.

In Turkey's case, a better understanding of fiscal sustainability may require extending the traditional analysis beyond fiscal composition considerations. For starters, a stable political backdrop is critical. A supportive institutional setup—aided by wide-ranging structural reforms—also appears central to the sustainability of fiscal adjustment efforts in Turkey. Nevertheless, if the country's fiscal adjustment efforts are to be sustained over the medium term, greater attention will likely need to be devoted to compositional issues, especially in controlling current expenditures.

IX Bank Restructuring and Financial Sector Reform

Mats Josefsson and David Marston

The Turkish banking system was highly concentrated at the end of the 1990s. Three large state banks represented about 27 percent of total assets, while the five largest private banks accounted for almost 40 percent. The remaining one-third of the system was made up of other private domestic banks (14 percent), intervened banks (12 percent), foreign branches (3 percent), and investment banks (5 percent).

A combination of weak banking practices, poor regulation, and lack of corporate governance had increased the vulnerability of the banking system. Most private banks were not publicly traded and many were run as de facto treasuries of their corporate groups. Throughout the 1990s, banks were relatively free to lend to their owners and to related companies (reflecting lax definitions of related parties and ample limits in relation to capital). Relaxed accounting rules in general and loan valuation rules in particular also allowed banks to inflate asset values and overstate their capital. Many of these private banks had heavily borrowed short-term funds in international capital markets and invested them in longer maturities in either government securities or loans to insiders or related parties, making them vulnerable to interest rate and exchange rate shocks.

The operations of state banks posed particular difficulties. Public banks were allocated to political parties for the purpose of providing subsidized credit to political constituencies. Bank losses generated by this activity were to be covered by the government. Rather than receiving income-earning assets, however, the banks booked claims on the government (duty losses). The accumulation of such duty losses made these banks highly vulnerable to liquidity and interest rate shocks. Chronic undercapitalization added to the distortions (Table 9.1).

Concerned about the supervisory weaknesses that had allowed these vulnerabilities to develop, the government took steps in mid-2000 to establish a legal and regulatory framework consistent with European Union and international standards. A revised banking law strengthened loan classification, loan loss provisioning, and collateral valuation rules. Loan concentration exposure limits were introduced; connected lending rules were defined, foreign currency exposure rules were tightened; new rules for consolidation, risk management, fitness, and propriety of owners and managers were established; and new accounting standards were set. New rules were also introduced to facilitate the exit of banks that were insolvent or illiquid. Prudential rules for private banks were extended to the state banks. An independent Banking Regulation and Supervision Agency (BRSA) was established in September 2000, and the Savings Deposit Insurance Fund (SDIF), which had been managed previously by the Central Bank of Turkey, was transferred under the BRSA.

Crisis Outbreak and Containment

In late 2000, disturbances in international capital markets and deteriorating economic conditions in Turkey resulted in significant losses in the banking system. During the year, deposit maturities shortened while consumer lending grew rapidly, with longer maturities and fixed interest rates. This widening maturity gap exposed banks to significant interest rate risk. Exposure of the state banks was particularly large, as they had become dependent on overnight funding. A sharp increase in domestic interest rates in late 2000 dramatically reduced bank profitability. In November 2000, Demirbank, a medium-sized financial institution, was unable to roll over its overnight liabilities and liquidated large quantities of government securities. The ensuing collapse in the value of government bonds prompted creditors to refuse to roll over overnight credit, resulting in a capital outflow and a sharp fall in Turkey's international reserves.

In response to these developments, the authorities introduced a strengthened economic policy package in December 2000, supported by an augmented program from the International Monetary Fund. The package made the implicit guarantee protecting depositors and other bank creditors explicit until the banking system had been rehabilitated. Specific loan provisions were also made tax deductible. The financial crisis eased temporarily. The key vulnerability indicators, how-

Table 9.1. Precrisis Vulnerabilities in the Banking System, December 2000

	In Billions of U.S. Dollars	In Percent of Capital
Foreign currency open positions	18.2	3,300
Accumulated duty losses in state banks	19.0	3,400
Short-term liabilities of state banks	22.4	4,100

ever, remained weak and the deeper problems were left unaddressed.

In February 2001, a much more serious crisis erupted that resulted in substantial losses for the banking system. Despite the December 2000 package, investor confidence was still shaky, reflecting the continued deterioration in the economy and weak policy implementation. The February crisis was ignited by the public airing of tensions between the president and the prime minister. Fearing a reversal of the stabilization policies, investors withdrew from the Turkish market. The resulting increase in domestic interest rates led to substantial losses, particularly for the state banks. The Central Bank of Turkey declared a two-day bank holiday, but when banks reopened, overnight interest rates spiked to about 5,000 percent. While Central Bank liquidity injections reduced interest rates to 700 percent, the magnitude of the injection destabilized the crawling peg exchange rate regime. The authorities were forced to float the Turkish lira on February 22, 2001, to avoid further loss of reserves. Deposit runs were averted because of the blanket guarantee protecting depositors and other creditors in banks (except share-holders' equity and subordinated debt), which had been made explicit the month before.

Bank Restructuring Strategy

A strengthened stabilization plan was introduced on May 15, 2001, to address, among other things, the financial sector's more fundamental weaknesses. The worsening economic environment and prospects for larger loan losses than earlier envisaged prompted authorities to refocus their strategy to deal with the core part of the banking system, which up until then had been considered sound. The revised banking sector strategy included the restructuring of the state banks, resolution of the SDIF banks, strengthening of the capital position of private banks, and asset management.

State Banks

The overnight exposure of public banks (state- and SDIF-owned intervened banks) was a major source of vulnerability in the banking system. The rollover of these liabilities at very high interest rates resulted in sharply growing losses and liquidity problems. As part of the restructuring of state banks, the government injected about $19 billion (13 percent of GNP) of securities into the state banks to eliminate the duty losses.

Two state banks (Ziraat and Halk) were operationally and financially restructured, while one insolvent bank (Emlak) was liquidated. Through the injection of $2.9 billion (2 percent of GNP) in government securities, the capital adequacy ratios of Ziraat and Halk were raised above the 8 percent regulatory requirement. Emlak had its license revoked and its banking assets and liabilities were transferred to Ziraat. Ziraat and Halk were operationally restructured and by end-2003, 820 branches had been closed and the number of employees reduced by 30,000 (Table 9.2).

Table 9.2. Operational Restructuring of Ziraat and Halk

	March 2001	June 2002	December 2002	December 2003	Difference[1]
Number of branches					
Ziraat	1,673	1,141	1,139	1,131	−542
Halk	805	549	546	527	−278
Total	2,478	1,690	1,685	1,658	−820
Number of personnel					
Ziraat	45,132	22,923	22,099	21,794	−23,338
Halk	14,699	14,956	8,300	7,993	−6,706
Total	59,831	37,879	30,399	29,787	−30,044

[1]December 2003 versus March 2001.

In addition, the separate boards of Ziraat and Halk were replaced by a joint board of professional bankers with instructions to restructure their operations in preparation for privatization. The resulting privatization plan addressed how to scale down the banks' holdings of government securities and increase their operational efficiency. The plan also took into account Ziraat's important role as a provider of rural banking services.

SDIF Banks

There has been substantial consolidation of the banking system in Turkey over the past several years (Table 9.3). Since 1997, 21 private banks have been taken over by the SDIF, 18 of them since December 1999. Most were relatively small, but altogether they accounted for 20 percent of banking system assets. Although efforts to privatize the banks did not always succeed, as of end-April 2004, the SDIF had been successful in resolving all of them except one, which has acted as a bridge bank. Resolution methods included merger (seven banks), liquidation (seven banks), and privatization (six banks).

Private Banking Sector

The authorities' initial strategy was to require proper valuation of bank assets and have shareholders recapitalize undercapitalized banks. In July 2001, six banks were unable to raise needed capital and were taken over by the BRSA. About a dozen other undercapitalized banks were required to strengthen their capital base through increases in paid-in capital, mergers, or participation of foreign investors. About $1.1 billion of new capital was raised. However, the authorities thought that these efforts were insufficient.

To protect the core private banking system, the authorities then introduced a support scheme that made public funds available to help banks recapitalize. They believed that banks would face additional losses given the adverse economic environment and would not be able to raise needed capital on their own. A public support scheme was therefore developed to ensure the solvency of the banking system and the continued confidence of depositors and other creditors. The scheme was designed to maximize private sector participation and limit the costs to the public sector (Box 9.1).

As a precursor to the recapitalization exercise, private banks were subject to a special audit. The objective was to identify all existing losses through a rigorous and targeted valuation exercise, and to ensure that this exercise was seen as transparent and technically sound. Particular emphasis was placed on establishing guidelines for the technical assessments, and on the choice of auditors to carry out the assessments and the third parties to conduct the back-up evaluations of the auditor assessments. Once the audit reports were submitted, the BRSA would recommend a course of action to any banks that required additional capital.

The public support scheme was completed by August 2002. Only one bank (the state-owned Vakifbank) needed Tier 2 capital assistance from the SDIF, amounting to $137 million. One other bank (Pamukbank) was intervened, since the owners could not raise about $2 billion in capital needed. The low demand for public resources reflected the incentives built into the program for shareholders to invest their own resources rather than to give the SDIF a role in managing their bank (Table 9.4).

Asset Management

Despite many attempts, the sale of assets of intervened banks has been slow. Nonperforming assets of intervened banks or assets that were rejected by the acquirers of former intervened banks were transferred to a

Table 9.3. Structure of the Banking System

	2000	2001	2002	2003
Number of branches	80	68	54	50
State	4	3	3	3
Savings Deposit Insurance Fund	11	9	2	2
Private	29	20	20	18
Foreign and investment banks	36	33	29	27
Market shares (in percent)	100	100	100	100
State	35	32	32	33
Savings Deposit Insurance Fund	11	6	4	3
Private	48	55	56	57
Foreign and investment banks	6	7	8	7

Box 9.1. Elements of the Bank Recapitalization Program

Public sector recapitalization programs must be designed taking into account specific circumstances and government policies. Not all programs will be alike. The availability of shareholder resources, the extent of recapitalization needed, and the legal structure will all affect program design. In 2001, Turkey initiated a public sector recapitalization program that included the criteria and conditions listed below.

Last resort: A public solvency support scheme should be viewed as a last option when there are no other alternatives available.

Private participation: For a bank to be eligible for public support, existing shareholders or new private investors must be willing to inject at least half of the Tier 1 capital needed.

Operational restructuring: To qualify for support, banks must present an acceptable operational restructuring plan, including measures to strengthen internal control and risk management, increase revenues, cut costs, and deal with nonperforming loans.

No bailout of existing shareholders: Capital needs in banks must be thoroughly assessed and all losses imposed on existing shareholders before public funds are injected. The assessment of capital needs should be verified by a third party. Ideally, the shares held by the government should have preferred status to shares held by the old shareholders. Thus, if there are additional losses over a given period of time, say six months, those losses should be absorbed by the old shareholders.

Positive net worth: To be eligible for support, a bank must have a positive net worth. If not, existing owners or new private investors must bring the capital adequacy ratio (CAR) to above zero before a bank can be eligible for public support.

Shareholders' rights: The government should have the right to appoint at least one board member irrespective of its capital contribution. Such board member(s), who should have documented experience in banking, should have veto powers on matters material to the soundness of the bank.

Price: The government should pay net book value for the shares. There is also a provision for buybacks. When the government wants to sell its shares, existing shareholders should have the right of first refusal for a given period, say two years. The price should be the highest of (i) the government's investment cost (principal and interest); (ii) net book value; and (iii) market price (including third-party offers).

Pledge: To protect the public investment, majority shareholders in the bank should be required to pledge as collateral to the government shares held in the bank equal to the government's capital contribution. The shares will be used as collateral if the government faces losses when it sells its shares in the bank.

Payment: The government should pay for the shares in tradable government bonds issued on market terms.

Convertibility: If the government provides Tier 2 capital, it should automatically be converted into Tier 1 capital if the CAR falls below a certain ratio, say 8 percent, and the private shareholders do not immediately bring it up to above 8 percent.

---

special collection department within the SDIF, while performing assets were transferred to Bayindirbank, which acted as a bridge bank. The IMF and the World Bank provided technical assistance to the SDIF collection department regarding the best procedures to maximize the values of these assets and to minimize the cost to the taxpayer for bank restructuring. Special legislation was also passed which gave the SDIF strong powers to recover the assets of former bank owners. Despite all these efforts, the first auction

Table 9.4. Financial Indicators for Private Banks
(In percent)

	2000	2001	2002	2003
Capital adequacy	18.3	9.0	19.6	23.5
Nonperforming loans/total loans	3.5	27.6	8.9	6.5
Provisions/nonperforming loans	63.0	31.0	53.0	80.0
Return on assets	2.3	−7.5	2.0	2.1
Return on equity	16.2	−97.9	15.9	13.9
Net profit (trillions of lira)	1,276	−7,383	2,409	2,917

of loans held by the SDIF was only completed in August 2004.

The separation of the SDIF and BRSA boards should help the SDIF focus on asset recovery. The new SDIF board established in January 2004 made it a priority to reassess the value of its assets in order to ensure that unrealistic expectations about recovery rates would not prevent asset sales. The new board also initiated development of a revised strategy for the resolution of assets of intervened banks, including claims against former bank owners and shares and companies taken over. The first asset disposal auction was completed in August 2004.

Corporate Restructuring

The market-based and voluntary scheme for corporate debt restructuring that was set up to strengthen the asset quality of banks is coming to an end. Loans that were classified on January 31, 2002, are eligible for restructuring under the Istanbul approach, provided certain conditions are met. An application for having the loans restructured must be submitted within three years (January 31, 2005) and all restructurings must be completed before June 2005, when the Framework Agreement on Financial Restructuring that governs the Istanbul approach expires. As of end-April 2004, 270 firms had $5.6 billion in loans restructured (Table 9.5), and nine applications totaling about $600 million were still pending. A significant amount of the restructuring is concentrated in a few groups. Of the group of large firms, 47 percent of the debt restructured ($5 billion) was owed by one group, while for smaller firms, 66 percent ($600 million) belonged to one group.

The outcome of these restructurings is still unclear, since significant grace periods have been granted. Restructuring was typically done by extending maturities and granting grace periods. For larger firms, the matu-

rity was extended to nine years on average, with an average grace period of more than 34 months to repay the principal and 22 months to honor interest rate payments. Thus, it will take roughly until mid-2005 before the first indications are available as to whether borrowers will be able to fulfill their commitments, or if most of the loans will turn nonperforming again. Moreover, the success of the Istanbul approach will to a large extent depend on the repayment capacity of one group, whose loan dominates.

Outcome of the Bank Rehabilitation Program

The authorities have been successful in resolving the immediate problems facing the banking system. The measures to prevent destabilization of the financial system—including the blanket guarantee to depositors and other creditors, elimination of short-term liabilities of public and intervened private banks, resolution of intervened banks, and implementation of prudential regulations in line with European Union standards—all achieved their objective. The authorities were also successful in recapitalizing private banks, which have now returned to profitability and have the financial resources to support the real sector and contribute to economic growth.

However, the cost to the government of restructuring the banking system amounted to about $47 billion (32 percent of GNP). This includes $6 billion to compensate depositors in Imar and an estimated $2 billion for the recapitalization of Pamukbank. Public sector costs have been borne primarily through the issuance of government securities. Government debt rose substantially as a result of the debt swap in restructuring the state banks ($22 billion or 15 percent of GNP) and the resolution of intervened banks ($25 billion or 17 percent of GNP). On average, banks hold about 43 percent of their assets in government securities (state banks hold 70 percent) and banking system solvency in the medium term is therefore tied to the success of the government's fiscal program and the country's economic performance.

The banking system's capital position and profitability have improved substantially in recent years. With the economic recovery and some loan restructuring, nonperforming loans have declined to an average of 7 percent for private banks (12 percent for the system). Capital adequacy ratios have grown from 19 to 24 percent in private banks (32 percent for the system) and return on equity increased in the system to an average of 9 percent by end-2003. Despite the increase in lending to the private sector in the past year, however, both assets (53 percent) and earnings (47 percent) are still concentrated in the holdings of government

Table 9.5. Loans Restructured Under the Istanbul Approach, as of April 2004

	Large Firms	Small Firms	Total
	(In millions of U.S. dollars)		
Amount	5,000	582	5,582
Of which:	*(In percent)*		
Private banks	63	88	66
Public banks	18	10	17
Savings Deposit Insurance Fund	14	1	12
Other	5	1	5
Total	100	100	100

securities. Thus the banks remain highly sensitive to the financial position of the government.

Stress tests indicate that banks' high capital adequacy ratios (CARs) now provide a significant cushion to shocks. While banks have a small short open position, banks accounting for 87 percent of system assets would remain solvent even if there were a 30 percent devaluation. Interest margins are adequate and all banks could withstand a 500-basis point reduction in margins. The system is least resilient to a deterioration in asset quality, but even here, given the levels of provisioning in the system, if 25 percent of performing loans were to become bad, banks accounting for 83 percent of the system would remain solvent. The system is also resilient to a combined shock of a depreciation and associated deterioration of asset quality. Stress tests indicate that this dual shock would leave system-wide CARs at around 20 percent.

In view of the improvements in the financial sector, the BRSA announced in July 2003 that the blanket guarantee protecting all depositors and creditors in banks would be replaced by a limited deposit protection scheme, which was implemented in July 2004. The authorities have decided to replace the guarantee in one step, rather than phasing it out. Under the new scheme, savings deposits up to TL 50 billion ($37,000) will be fully protected (about 40 percent of total deposits). Before the guarantee was abolished, the BRSA informed the government in detail about the condition of the banking system and of any remaining risks that the banks might face. A summary of these findings was published.

The SDIF's losses need to be recognized. To finance the resolution of intervened banks, the SDIF has had to borrow a substantial amount of government securities from the Treasury. As of end-December 2003, SDIF liabilities amounted to $36.2 billion, including $13.6 billion of accrued interest. Recapitalization of Pamukbank would add another $2 billion. It is highly unlikely the SDIF will ever be able to repay the Treasury the full amount through asset resolution or the collection of deposit insurance fees. Thus, the Treasury will have to write off its claims on the SDIF. To create confidence and to ensure that the SDIF will be able to meet all its commitments, there are benefits to providing this up front.

Challenges Ahead

With crisis resolution having been successful, implementation of medium-term structural measures should now be at the center of the agenda. Structural issues such as the privatization of state banks, asset sales, correcting weaknesses in the legal system, and reducing distortionary taxes have been delayed. Addressing these issues will enhance confidence in the financial system and complete the reforms.

State Banks

Restructuring and privatization of the three state banks—Ziraat, Halk, and Vakif—has proved difficult. Progress has been limited because of the banks' high exposure to government securities and political uncertainties, which have discouraged outside buyers (Table 9.6). Vakif is conducting its own diligence as a first step toward diluting its existing ownership through a public offering of new shares. Halk has been integrated with Pamuk, which should enhance its information and computer systems, and strengthen its competence in providing banking services. For Ziraat, any privatization strategy would need to respect its social function, since in many rural areas it is the sole provider of banking services. For each of the state banks, the need to improve the balance sheet structure, especially the predominance of government bonds, is a key challenge for successful privatization.

Asset Recovery

The sale of assets of the intervened banks has proceeded very slowly. For the most part, this can be explained by (i) lower than hoped for recovery rates, (ii) the need to make more realistic asset valuations, and (iii) the poor legal protection for BRSA and SDIF staff in the event that they are accused of selling assets below value. In addition, the considerable overlap between the compositions of the BRSA and SDIF boards may have weakened the SDIF's focus. The decision to appoint a new and independent SDIF board in January 2004 should overcome this difficulty and help speed up asset sales.

Table 9.6. Assets and Liabilities of Ziraat and Halk
(In percent)

	2001	2002	2003
Assets	**100**	**100**	**100**
Liquid assets	11	9	13
Nonperforming loans	2	1	2
Holdings of securities	69	74	0
Loan portfolio	7	5	70
Other assets	11	11	10
Liabilities	**100**	**100**	**100**
Deposits	70	76	77
Interbank	7	5	3
Equity, including profit	9	11	13
Other liabilities	14	8	7
Market share in lending	8	7	8
Market share in deposits	29	30	32

Legal Underpinnings

The final ruling by the General Assembly of the Administrative Court on April 24, 2004 that BRSA's interventions in Demirbank and Kentbank were unlawful has complicated bank resolution. However, the consequences of the ruling are unclear, since the banks have since been taken over or liquidated (Demirbank was intervened in December 2000 and Kentbank in July 2001). This unpredictability undermines bank reform.

A commission has been established to look into the supervisory lessons from the Imar bank failure. Imar collapsed after the operating licenses of energy companies held by its owners were confiscated. Subsequent investigations revealed that the bank had $5.5 billion in unregistered but legitimate deposits that were not backed by assets on the bank's balance sheet. The scandal weakened the BRSA's credibility and raised questions about supervisory practices, including how the bank was able to operate like this for so many years. To avoid any repetition and to determine the supervisory lessons from the experience, the government set up a commission, chaired by a reputable international bank supervisor, which reported its findings in August 2004 (Box 9.2).

In response, the authorities are revising the Banking Act to bring it more closely in line with European Union standards and international best practices (Box 9.3). The need for such a comprehensive review has been brought to the fore by the experience of crisis management over the last few years, the separation of the boards of the BRSA and the SDIF, lessons from the Imar scandal, and the court rulings making the intervention in two banks unlawful. Lacking a review of the act, weaknesses in the judicial system could undermine banking reform and deter foreign investment.

Box 9.2. The Imar Commission Report

After the failure of the Imar Bank, the government formed an independent commission to assess the supervisory lessons that should be learned from the scandal. The commission consisted of Jean-Louis Fort, former director general of the Banking Commission in France, and Peter Hayward, former secretary of the Basel Committee on Banking Supervision. In its report published in August 2004, the commission noted three requirements of any effective supervisory authority: a sound legal basis, adequate financial and human resources, and an effective organizational structure. To help meet these requirements, the commission recommended the following legislative changes:

- Board members appointed to banks by the Banking Regulation and Supervision Agency (BRSA), should act as representatives of that agency and not as regular directors of the bank. The BRSA should also have the right to remove and appoint new members of the executive and auditing boards of such banks.
- The powers to conduct onsite examination and to request information should belong to the BRSA as a whole and not exclusively to sworn bank auditors. The commission argued that expertise and experience found elsewhere among BRSA staff should be used in onsite examinations. The legal requirement that only sworn bank auditors can perform onsite work removes a desirable element of flexibility, including the need to use outside expertise, and this can hinder effective supervision.
- The role of the sworn bank auditors as tax auditors should be removed. The commission stated that "this is an extremely unusual element" and that in most countries it is felt important that supervisors should have no responsibilities in this area.
- External auditors should have the right to inform the BRSA of their findings.

- Overly detailed legislation would reduce the flexibility of the BRSA. Detailed application of general requirements should be left to secondary legislation or regulations in a way that can be easily altered to meet changes in the market environment.

The commission also suggested ways to strengthen the BRSA's day-to-day operations. Regarding resources, the commission found that BRSA has an insufficient number of staff with experience in banking, external audit, information technology, trading, and back office operations. The skill base could be strengthened by broadening the recruitment base, implementing a more flexible pay structure, creating short- and medium-term assignments, and seconding staff from the private sector.

In the organizational area, the commission firmly stressed the importance of better coordination of onsite and offsite supervision. According to the commission, officers from the offsite department should be given overall responsibility either for the supervision of one large bank or a group of smaller banks. The officer should ensure full communications between various functions in BRSA, prepare briefs and determine areas for inspection, follow up on corrective actions, and coordinate with external auditors.

Regarding the BRSA's governance structure, accountability should be pushed down from the chairman to the officers in charge of supervision of individual banks. Procedures should also be in place that allow the board to assess the performance of the agency and its staff, including external reviews of BRSA's efficiency.

There might also be scope for improving the performance of the BRSA board. The status of board members should be reviewed, particularly the appointment of full-time board members without executive functions. Consideration should be given to appointing at least some part-time members with private sector experience.

Box 9.3. Priority Areas for Legal Reform

Scope of legislation: The Banking Act needs to specify the types of business operations that fall within the scope of the legislation and which require a banking license. Moreover, once a banking license is issued, the law should clearly define the permissible banking activities in which a bank can engage.

Fit and proper criteria: The current act establishes "fit and proper" requirements generally consistent with international best practices. The key issue is to make sure that these criteria are not weakened in any way.

Criteria for licensing: The current act does not clearly specify the criteria that the Banking Regulation and Supervision Agency (BRSA) should employ in determining whether to approve or disapprove an application for a new bank authorization.

Large exposure limits: The application of the transitional arrangements allowing large exposure limits to exceed the limit of 25 percent of the bank's own funds is not consistent with international best practices. The authorities intend to phase out these transitional arrangements by end-2005.

Lending to related parties: The limits on lending to related parties are not consistent with international

best practices and need to be strengthened by broadening their scope of coverage.

Onsite inspections: The exclusivity of sworn bank auditors to examine banks should be abolished and BRSA given the right to use other experts (both internal and external experts) as well to conduct onsite inspections.

Legal protection for board members and staff of BRSA and the Savings Deposit Insurance Fund (SDIF): The Banking Act needs to be amended to fully protect board members and staff of these agencies from liability for actions taken in good faith in the normal course of their duties. Moreover, the BRSA and SDIF should be required by law to indemnify these individuals for legal expenses incurred in defending against civil actions or criminal prosecutions that are ultimately unsuccessful.

Delineation of BRSA and SDIF responsibilities: With the split of the BRSA and SDIF boards, the delineation of responsibilities between the two agencies will need to be addressed, including the resolution of insolvent banks, the operation of the deposit insurance scheme, and how to protect the independence of the agencies, particularly from unwarranted interference by the government and the judiciary.

Intermediation Capacity

Distortionary taxes on financial transactions—including the Banking Insurance and Transactions Tax (BITT), the Resource Utilization and Support Fund (RUSF), and a range of stamp duties—have increased loan-to-deposit spreads by approximately 10 percentage points during the period of high interest rates. The government's weak fiscal position has made it difficult to eliminate these taxes, which discourage bank-financed investment and encourage offshore operations (Figure 9.1). Some stamp duties were abolished on January 1, 2004, but there is also a need to reduce the BITT and RUSF, although in a phased and gradual manner.

To circumvent these tax-induced spreads, loans are being booked in offshore branches of resident banks. The wedge in effective lending rates has amplified the role of offshore subsidiaries of domestic banks in the intermediation process. To avoid paying the BITT, RUSF, and some stamp duties, and to circumvent regulations governing bank lending in foreign currency, most large banks have established offshore branches to intermediate credits to onshore Turkish corporations. Branches for this purpose are mostly incorporated in Malta and Bahrain, and credit expansion is financed primarily through transfers from the onshore

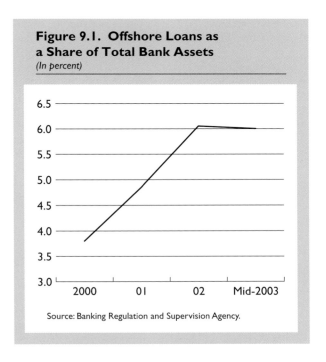

Figure 9.1. Offshore Loans as a Share of Total Bank Assets
(In percent)

Source: Banking Regulation and Supervision Agency.

headquarters. Credit on the consolidated balance sheet of banks with offshore banks has grown by 70 percent in the past three years. Loans booked offshore have increased by 260 percent.

The characteristics of deposits are also being adapted. Banks are increasingly offering deposit instruments that, while contractually long term, take advantage of the associated lower withholding tax but have all the other characteristics of one-month deposits in terms of liquidity and repricing. To maintain the attractiveness of deposits compared to investing directly in government securities, banks offer investment (mutual fund) type facilities (Type B investment funds). Through this vehicle, depositors take advantage of the income tax exemption for mutual funds to realize higher yields.

The extensive use of transaction taxes in Turkey is a major obstacle to the development of a more diversified financial system. The costs of circumventing these may favor larger banks over smaller ones and discriminate against the establishment of nonbank financial institutions such as leasing and factoring companies. To avoid paying stamp duties, banks reportedly enter into informal arrangements rather than documented transactions, which weakens legal compliance.

Lessons Learned

A number of important lessons can be gleaned from Turkey's postcrisis restructuring exercise:

1. **Costs could have been lower:**
   - *Resolution of intervened banks.* Although all intervened banks have now been resolved, the initial process was slow. Banks taken over in the late 1990s were not resolved until late 2001 and in some cases even later. Initially, delays were caused by the authorities' reluctance to liquidate banks or by unrealistic expectations about privatization values. Laws and weaknesses in the judicial system also contributed. If a firm policy on dealing with intervened banks had been in place (for example, auctioning off assets and liabilities if the bank could not be sold in a fixed time), the cost of bank restructuring might have been much lower.
   - *Asset sales.* Roughly three years after the peak of the crisis, only limited amounts of money have been recovered. The main reasons for the delay have been a lack of willingness by the authorities to sell the assets because they feared low recovery rates, and the lack of legislation to protect staff and board members from lawsuits. These delays will almost certainly increase the final cost. The lesson is to fully incorporate asset management in the bank restructuring strategy and make sure there are no legal problems in selling the assets.

2. **Legal risks could have been addressed earlier:**
   - *Legal system.* Despite weaknesses in the legal system, the BRSA successfully intervened and resolved 21 banks. Much can be achieved in bank restructuring even under a weak legal system, provided the supervisory agency is willing to take action. Clearly, the BRSA's responsibility and willingness to take such action to solve the banking problems saved money. With a more predictable legal system, the cost might have been even lower. The legal weaknesses have also invited political interference, pressure from interest groups, and conflicts of interest that have affected BRSA and SDIF activities. With hindsight, the lack of predictability in the legal system should have been addressed earlier, although the extent of the problem only became clear in the course of the reform.

3. **Timely public information was critical:**
   - *Keeping the public informed.* The BRSA made a considerable effort to keep the public informed—in the recapitalization exercise, for example, a special brochure explained in simple terms what the exercise was all about, which kept depositors calm. Although 21 banks have been taken over, confidence in the financial system has been maintained.

4. **Notwithstanding major successes, the supervisory structure was deficient:**
   - *Close cooperation between onsite and offsite supervision.* The Imar banking scandal is an example of supervisory failure, and the Imar Commission identified lack of coordination between offsite and onsite supervision as a key cause. In addition, because it is difficult for even the most qualified examiner to detect fraud, the supervisory agency must have the right to bring in outside expertise, when needed, to participate in onsite examinations. In the case of the Imar scandal, an information technology and forensic audit might have revealed the misreporting.
   - *Separation of BRSA and SDIF.* The institutional overlap between these two agencies, with both having almost the same board, was a source of considerable distraction. The postcrisis push to rehabilitate the banking system and dispose of its bad assets, in a context of substantial legal uncertainty, required a greater degree of specialization and resources to have successfully implemented both.

5. **Most important is incentive design—sticks and carrots work:**
   - *Recapitalization.* When sufficient pressure is put on banks to raise capital and when there also is an alternative through the use of public funds,

shareholders are likely to put in the capital needed. The public support scheme provided assistance to the SDIF based on well-defined criteria, and included disincentives for incumbents to seek SDIF recapitalization assistance.

While all of these lessons are important, and though there are many reforms still to be implemented, Turkey's banking system is today much stronger than during the crisis. The economy is recovering and banks are better positioned to support and contribute to economic growth. Net profits of private banks rose by more than 20 percent in 2003, and with the decline in real interest rates, bank lending to the private sector has started to increase. To ensure the banking system's continued strength, the key now is to maintain and build upon the financial sector reforms introduced over the last three years.

X   Labor Market Developments[1]

Mathew Verghis

Population growth has outpaced employment growth for many years in Turkey, dating as far back as the 1960s. Taking just the period from 1980–2003, the working-age population grew by 20 million, but only 3.4 million jobs were created (Figure 10.1). As a result, by 2003, Turkey's employment rate of 43.2 percent—that is, the percentage of the adult population that is employed— was one of the lowest in the world. Most countries, with exceptions largely in the Middle East, have employment rates in excess of 50 percent. The European Union average was 63 percent in 2002.

The unemployment rate, at 10.3 percent in 2003, is not as much of an outlier as the employment rate by European standards. The discrepancy is because of one of the striking features of the Turkish labor market, which is the low labor force participation rate. Figure 10.1 shows the increasing divergence between the adult population and the labor force—a growing share of people not employed were not looking for work and thus not counted as unemployed. As will be seen in the next two sections, low labor force participation is particularly pronounced for women. Both supply and demand considerations are also factors.

Low wages have kept Turkish labor costs internationally competitive. Labor value added, at $7,345 in 2002, was relatively low, but so was labor compensation at $2,297 (Table 10.1). The labor cost per unit value-added of 0.31 is substantially less than the other European Union and accession comparators. However, the increase between 1995 and 2002 in Turkey's labor costs per unit value added in manufacturing and services—5 percent and 4.2 percent, respectively—was substantially higher than any of the other comparators.

Real wage growth has been well below labor productivity growth since the mid-1990s. During the first half of that decade, real wages outpaced labor productivity by a wide margin (Figure 10.2). Following the economic crisis in 1994, real wages fell sharply and then remained relatively constant, with some fluctuation. Real wages fell sharply again in 2001 following another economic crisis. Wages started to recover in

2003, but at the end of the year were still 15 percent below end-2000 levels. Labor productivity has been on an increasing trend consistent with the steady transformation of the economy from low-productivity agriculture to higher-productivity sectors. More recently, this trend also reflects falling real wages and an increase in average working hours.

A strong legal framework to protect the rights of workers does not protect workers against risks of unemployment and income loss. This framework includes the Social Security system, labor legislation that restricts the rights of employers to fire workers, unemployment insurance, and proactive labor market policies. In practice, however, relatively few workers have access to the mandated social protection, and one effect of this system appears to be a growing informal sector. Depending on the data source, from 42 to 49 percent of the employed labor force belongs to one of the Social Security organizations. Coverage is higher in urban areas at 63 percent. Unemployment insurance is available to about 20 percent of the employed workforce. Employment protection laws such as severance payments are reported to be widely flouted. While the informal sector contributes to the flexibility of the labor market, it brings down aggregate productivity and contributes to the imbalances in the Social Security system.

Labor Supply

The ongoing demographic transition in Turkey has led to a significant increase in the working-age population. This has generated large numbers of young, inexperienced workers who have been difficult to absorb into productive employment. Population growth slowed from 2.7 percent in 1950 to 1.6 percent currently, and is expected to be near zero in 2050 (Table 10.2). However, because of the falling infant mortality rate, the age structure of the population becomes skewed toward younger ages.

The fertility rate fell from 6.9 per 1,000 population in 1950–55 to around 2.4 currently, and is expected to decline slightly further to a little over 2 within the next five to 10 years. But the population is expected to continue to

---

[1]This chapter draws on an upcoming study of the labor market in Turkey by the World Bank in cooperation with Turkish authorities.

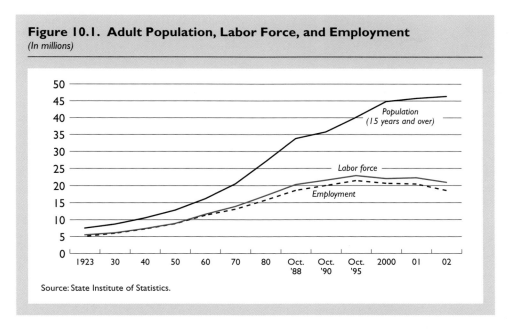

Figure 10.1. Adult Population, Labor Force, and Employment
(In millions)

Population
(15 years and over)

Labor force

Employment

Source: State Institute of Statistics.

grow beyond that point because of a disproportionate number of women of child bearing age, and eventually stabilize at around 100 million in the second half of the twenty-first century.

The bulge in the economically productive age group constitutes a demographic window of opportunity. For Turkey, the peak growth rate of the working-age population occurred in the early 1980s (Table 10.2), when an especially sharp surge coincided with a reversal in net migration. Working-age population growth in the range of 2.5 to 3 percent is rapid in historical perspective, and during 1980–2003, the total increase was 20.5 million persons. By 2020, more than 21 million new workers—today's under-15 cohort—will have reached working age. If the economy cannot generate productive jobs for these workers, the public policy challenge by 2050 will be to support the bulge in the population that will be dropping out of the labor force.

Table 10.1. International Competitiveness
(Labor cost per value-added unit in current U.S. dollars)

	2002		Total Economy			Agriculture			Manufacturing			Services, Including Public		
	Value added[1]	Compensation[1]	1995	2002	Percent change[2]	1995	2002	Percent change	1995	2002	Percent change	1995	2002	Percent change
Turkey	7,345	2,297	0.25	0.31	4.5	0.08	0.09	1.4	0.19	0.25	5.0	0.33	0.41	4.2
Portugal[3]	16,233	8,626	0.53	0.53	0.2	0.17	0.2	6.0	0.58	0.57	−0.2	0.56	0.55	−0.4
Spain	36,416	19,275	0.52	0.53	0.5	0.17	0.21	4.5	0.62	0.68	1.8	0.51	0.51	−0.1
Greece	29,654	10,902	0.35	0.37	1.0	0.09	0.11	4.9	0.50	0.46	−1.7	0.36	0.38	1.1
Poland	18,589	9,278	0.48	0.50	0.7	0.19	0.23	4.0	0.54	0.61	2.2	0.49	0.49	−0.2
Hungary[4]	9,755	5,060	0.53	0.52	−0.6	0.38	0.39	0.8	0.59	0.57	−0.6	0.53	0.51	−0.8
Mexico	15,750	5,544	0.32	0.35	1.8	0.17	0.19	1.8	0.27	0.32	3.1	0.35	0.37	1.3
Korea	33,544	15,179	0.47	0.45	−0.9	0.10	0.10	0.9	0.45	0.39	−2.9	0.52	0.50	−0.5

Source: Household Labor Force Survey; State Institute of Statistics; Organization for Economic Cooperation and Development, STructural ANalysis (STAN).
[1]Per employee, expressed in U.S. dollars.
[2]Compound average annual growth.
[3]Portugal data for 1995 and 1997 only.
[4]Data for 1995 and 2001 only.

Figure 10.2. Productivity and Real Wages in Private Manufacturing

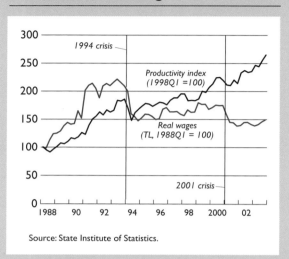

Source: State Institute of Statistics.

The quality of the work force as measured by educational attainment has been improving. The system of primary and secondary education provided free by the state was extensively revised in the late 1990s, and compulsory schooling was raised from five to eight years. Higher education opportunities also grew during the 1980s and 1990s through new universities, both public and private, and distance learning programs. Enrollment in higher education, though at comparatively low levels, registered strong gains, particularly for women. Results are apparent: a decline in the share of those who are illiterate or without basic education, a roughly constant share of those with primary education, and a rapidly growing share, though still small, of those with a higher education (Table 10.3).

Turkey still lags comparator countries in levels of human capital. The secondary enrollment rate is 58 percent compared to an average of 67.9 percent for middle-income countries and 67.7 percent for Middle Eastern and North African countries. Turkey also lags Eastern Europe, including the new European Union members where education systems are already at near industrial country levels.

High unemployment rates for educated youth suggest that there is not yet sufficient demand for skilled labor. In 2002, unemployment was 45 percent for high school graduates and 31 percent for college graduates ages 20–24, but only 12 percent for primary school graduates. This probably reflects educated workers having a higher reservation wage. But it also reflects a paradox (also seen in many other countries): those who are educated and should be in high demand are unemployed. Not only does this have implications for productivity, it also creates considerable dissatisfaction among an important segment of the population. Over time, it may reduce the incentives to seek education.

Labor force participation in Turkey is exceptionally low by international standards and has been in long-term decline. The overall participation rate of 48.3 percent in 2003 was the lowest among member countries of the Organization for Economic Cooperation and Development (OECD) and 20 percentage points below the OECD av-

Table 10.2. Population Growth and Shares by Decade
(In percent)

	1950–60	1960–70	1970–80	1980–90	1990–2000	2000–10	2010–20	2020–30	2030–40	2040–50
					Growth rate					
0–14	3.4	2.3	2.2	1.2	0.2	−0.3	−0.6	−0.6	−0.3	−0.6
15–64	2.3	2.5	2.6	3.0	2.3	2.0	1.3	0.7	0.1	−0.2
65+	3.5	4.8	3.1	1.4	4.4	2.5	3.3	4.1	3.5	2.5
					Share					
0–14	41.2	42.2	41.2	38.6	34.1	29.1	24.9	21.4	19.4	17.9
15–64	55.5	53.9	54.4	57.1	61.0	65.0	68.2	69.4	68.0	65.7
65+	3.3	3.9	4.4	4.3	4.9	5.8	6.9	9.2	12.6	16.4
Memorandum items:										
15–64 population in less developed countries, excluding China										
Of which:										
Growth rate	2.0	2.3	2.7	2.7	2.4	2.2	1.7	1.3	0.9	0.6
Share	56.0	54.3	54.5	56.3	58.3	61.1	63.5	64.9	65.7	65.9

Source: United Nations Population Fund.

Table 10.3. Educational Attainment
(In percent of population)

	Total Population		Men		Women	
	1988	2001	1988	2001	1988	2001
Illiterate	22.9	13.4	11.6	5.4	33.9	21.4
No diploma	9.1	4.5	9.6	4.3	8.6	4.7
Primary	47.2	48.1	51.8	47.7	42.8	48.4
Junior	8.1	10.2	10.5	13.2	5.7	7.1
Junior vocational	0.7	0.2	1.0	0.2	0.5	0.2
High	6.0	10.7	7.1	12.7	5.0	8.6
High vocational	2.7	5.2	3.8	6.9	1.7	3.5
College+	3.2	5.7	4.7	7.2	1.8	4.2

Source: Household Labor Force Survey.

erage (Table 10.4). Participation and employment rates differ significantly with respect to gender and location. Rural participation rates are higher than urban ones, and men's rates are higher than women's. Women's labor force participation in urban areas, at only 18.6 percent, is exceptionally low, although educated urban women are much more likely than uneducated ones to participate in the labor force. For the overall economy, the male participation rate of 70.4 percent is nearly three times the female rate of 26.6 percent.

Labor Demand

The slow pace of employment generation has persisted despite relatively strong economic growth in Turkey. From 1980–2002, annual real GNP growth averaged about 4 percent, compared to employment growth of 0.8 percent (Table 10.5). Real per capita GNP growth, though not spectacular, averaged 2 percent, and per capita GNP in current U.S. dollars more than tripled, from $1,593 to $5,315.

Table 10.4. Labor Force Participation and Employment in 2003

	Population, 15+	Labor Force	Employment Rate	Participation	Employment Rate
	In millions			In percent	
Total	48.9	23.6	21.1	48.3	43.2
Of which:					
Female	24.7	6.6	5.9	26.6	23.9
Male	24.3	17.1	15.3	70.4	62.9
Urban	29.9	13.1	11.3	43.8	37.7
Of which:					
Female	14.9	2.8	2.3	18.6	15.1
Male	15.0	10.3	9.0	68.9	60.3
Rural	19.0	10.6	9.9	55.5	51.9
Of which:					
Female	9.7	3.8	3.6	39.0	37.4
Male	9.3	6.8	6.2	72.9	67.1
Memorandum item:					
OECD total[1]	...	...	...	69.4	64.1

Sources: State Institute of Statistics, Household Labor Force Survey. http://lmisnt.pub.die.gov.tr/die/plsql/lmwe beng.lmrapor_header.

[1]Data from *OECD Economic Outlook*, December 2003, is not strictly comparable to Household Labor Force Survey.

Table 10.5. Output, Employment, and Productivity Growth
(Average annual percent change)

	Output Per Worker		Growth Rate, 1980–2002			
	1980	2002	Output	Employment	Productivity	Contribution to Productivity Growth[1]
	(In 1987 U.S. dollars)		(In percent)			
Total	3,302	6,329	3.8	0.8	3.0	3.0
Agriculture	1,641	2,492	1.1	−0.8	1.9	1.0
Industry	6,059	10,045	5.2	2.8	2.3	0.3
Construction	3,946	6,537	2.5	0.2	2.3	0.1
Services	4,720	7,855	4.3	1.9	2.3	0.8

[1]Sectoral contributions calculated using 1980 shares of total employment as weights.

Slow employment growth may be partially explained by the decline in employment in the agriculture sector. Agriculture was the largest employer in 1980, accounting for 9 million jobs or 50 percent of the total. By 2002, agricultural employment had declined in absolute terms, shedding 1.6 million jobs to 7.4 million or 35 percent of the total. At the same time, despite a fall in output per capita, the sector continues to satisfy most domestic demand for crops and livestock, while supplying traditional exports such as dried fruits and nuts. Countries with large shares of agricultural jobs often generate employment more slowly because workers are concentrated in the slowest growing sector.

Industry and service sector jobs are likely to be the key to employment generation in the years ahead. Industry accounted for 2.1 million jobs in 1980, only 12 percent of the total, but showed the fastest growth over the period, adding 1.8 million jobs to reach 3.9 million in 2002. The sector consists mostly of manufacturing of a wide variety of outputs for both domestic and export markets, including cement, petrochemicals, steel, textiles and clothing, automotive parts, household durables, and consumer electronics. Export-oriented automotive and electronics products have been the fastest growing categories. Service employment also rose from 5.9 million to 9 million, with its share of employment rising from 33 to 41 percent. Tourism services are a major export earner, plus the sector also produces financial services, transportation, and trade earnings.

The pace of investment in manufacturing, however, has been slower than in other sectors. While private investment rose as a share of GNP following the reforms of the 1980s, much of this was associated with a speculative residential investment boom triggered by high inflation (Figure 10.3). By contrast, structural reforms had only a limited impact on manufacturing investment, which barely reached 5 percent of GNP in the mid-1990s before losing ground again during the ensuing crises. The recent increase in manufacturing investment is a positive sign.

While employment growth has been slow, aggregate employment does not appear to fall significantly, even during crises. In 1994, GNP fell by 6.3 percent while employment continued to grow. That may partly reflect a tendency for agriculture to act as a social safety net, as indicated by a sharp increase in agricultural employment in 1995. In 2001, GNP fell by 9.9 percent, while employment fell by just 0.8 percent. In this case, employment in industry and services continued to grow despite sharp declines in output in these sectors, and while employment

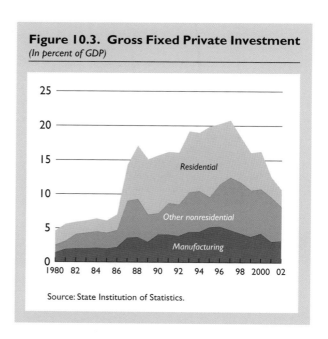

Figure 10.3. Gross Fixed Private Investment
(In percent of GDP)

Source: State Institution of Statistics.

in agriculture fell, the elasticity was not exceptionally high. The construction sector—which accounts for only 5 percent of GNP and employment—did shed a significant number of jobs in 2001 and 2002, though this is more likely related to the aftermath of the construction boom of the late 1990s than to any short-term volatility. There are widespread reports that employers are able to adjust informally to the crisis through measures such as unpaid leave.

Increased working hours partly explains the limited response of employment to growth. The number of hours worked per week is high in Turkey and has been increasing. Urban wage and salaried employees worked an average of 46 hours per week in 1988, and by 2001 this had increased to over 50 hours. Casual workers in urban areas were already working 56 hours a week in 1988 and this rose to 60 hours a week by 2001. This increase in working hours may also partially explain the measured increase in labor productivity. Employers and employees are choosing to respond to changes in business conditions by adjusting the number of hours rather than the number of workers.

Lowering the costs of hiring and firing workers may encourage employers to hire new workers as the economy expands. Under current regulations, the labor market may not be sufficiently flexible going forward (see below). In addition, as inflation declines, sustaining real wage adjustments will be more difficult. Further, there is a natural limit to increasing working hours rather than hiring new workers.

Labor Market Regulation

The Labor Code passed in May 2003 introduced important changes in the regulation of labor. Part-time and fixed-term contracts were placed on an equal legal footing with full-time and indeterminate forms of employment. Flexibility was introduced in terms of working time. Collective dismissals were regulated in detail for the first time. In the area of job security, there was increased protection for workers in firms with 30 or more employees.[2] The major changes brought about by the law for these workers are that employers cannot terminate a contract without just cause, and that the burden of proof rests with the employer. Courts or arbitrators may declare a termination invalid and order reinstatement of the worker with compensation.

---

[2]This threshold applies to an employer with at least 30 employees in the same industry, even where a particular workplace has less than 30 employees. The increased job security provisions only apply to indeterminate employees with at least six months in the workplace.

Statutory employment protection legislation remains costly by comparative standards. The cost of complying with the legislation (which includes severance pay and other regulations concerned with dismissal) is more than double the OECD average. The impact of these regulations is to create a duality in the labor market. They increase the stability of existing jobs, but at a price—more long-term unemployment and nonparticipation in the labor force and less opportunity for regular employment in the formal sector. This tends to increase the vulnerability of certain groups of workers, including women and youth who are less likely to get these "good" jobs. Many of these workers, then, will be relegated to the informal sector or out of the labor force.

Labor taxes are high and likely to encourage the informal sector. Social security, health insurance, and unemployment insurance premiums for regular workers—paid by both employees and employers—are between 36 and 42 percent of insurable earnings, depending on the occupational risk. Relative to wages, this forms a high tax rate when compared with other countries. It is also likely to be a key factor in moving employment to the informal sector. As discussed earlier, less than half the employed population belongs to one of the Social Security organizations, and there is believed to be widespread underreporting of earnings. International experience suggests that cutting rates will not, by itself, lead to be better compliance in the short term.

With a high premium and low payout, the unemployment insurance fund has a large surplus. Despite an increase in claimants in 2002 and early 2003—an increase which has since reached a plateau—the number of unemployment insurance beneficiaries remains small. Currently, less than 2 percent of unemployed workers are receiving benefits. A survey finds five Eastern European countries with coverage rates between 25 and 50 percent, and OECD countries with rates between 25 and 75 percent. Newly established unemployment insurance systems, such as those in Korea (14 percent) and Hong Kong SAR (8 percent), have coverage rates well above those of Turkey. The low level of coverage is explained partly by the extent of informality—only premium paying members who were registered as being laid off rather than having quit are eligible—and partly by tight eligibility criteria.

A carefully designed package of labor reforms currently being prepared by the World Bank in cooperation with Turkish authorities could help reconcile the two sometimes conflicting objectives of employment generation and worker protection. Such a package could include severance pay reform, unemployment insurance reform, proactive labor market policies, collective bargaining reform, job security regulations, and dispute resolution mechanisms.

XI Conclusions

Donal McGettigan and Reza Moghadam

Two key aspects of Turkey's economic performance emerge from the analysis presented in this paper. First, recovery from the 2000–01 crisis has been remarkable, led by sound macroeconomic policies and supported by an impressive array of structural reforms. Inflation has fallen to its lowest level in a generation, while the recovery in output has outperformed all expectations. Interest rates have fallen substantially and the Turkish lira has become a store of value. The successful redenomination of the lira has been a welcome consequence of the stabilization effort.

Second, despite this success, significant vulnerabilities remain, the key sources of which are the high levels and vulnerable structure of government and external debt. The financing outlook thus remains challenging, as short public debt maturities add to domestic rollover risk and the government faces high external debt repayments in the years ahead. A sudden shift in investor sentiment could pressure exchange and interest rates, in turn undermining disinflation and weakening bank and government balance sheets. The high current account deficit, financed largely by short-term inflows, adds to this concern. Another worry is the high unemployment rate. Despite the high rate of labor force growth and robust economic growth, employment generation has not yet been strong enough to significantly reduce unemployment.

Political developments have facilitated the reforms needed to underpin the stabilization effort. The severity of the 2000–01 crisis generated the political momentum to put in place sound macroeconomic policies and enact critical structural reforms. In addition, the formation of Turkey's first single-party majority government since the 1980s has provided a helpful backdrop for reform. Prospects for an ongoing, positive economic performance have benefited from political support for the creation of independent and strong institutions, strides made to improve transparency (especially in the fiscal area), and the wide range of legislative reforms in economic areas.

The analyses in this paper suggest several elements of a forward-looking reform agenda to sustain Turkey's improved economic performance and address the vulnerabilities that remain:

- **Primary surplus.** Sustained high primary surpluses have clearly been the key to the success of economic policies over the last few years. Sustained surpluses would facilitate higher growth and support ongoing disinflation efforts. This would also reduce Turkey's public debt burden to safer levels and help contain the current account deficit. On the financing side, shifting to longer-term local currency instruments should help lower the government's own balance sheet vulnerabilities.

- **Structural fiscal reforms.** Although successful to date, Turkey's fiscal adjustment efforts face the risk of unraveling unless they are supported by deeper structural reforms. These reforms should include controlling expenditures through such means as comprehensive Social Security and civil service reform. Improved tax administration and a streamlined tax system are needed to address tax evasion and broaden Turkey's narrow tax base.

- **Monetary policy.** The Central Bank's impressive disinflation record has been one of Turkey's major achievements in recent years. Continued disinflation would lay the foundation for sustained higher growth and, over time, should help reduce dollarization, a key balance sheet concern. In addition to sustained fiscal consolidation, credibility of the Central Bank itself is essential. The bank's recent moves toward formal inflation targeting should help, but safeguarding the institution's independence is also critical. On the external side, the Central Bank has also announced an ambitious reserve accumulation target that should help address Turkey's external balance sheet vulnerabilities.

- **Banking reforms.** Despite major achievements, further critical reforms of the banking sector are needed. Most importantly, the supervisory and legal framework needs to be brought closer to European Union standards, asset recovery accelerated, and state banks restructured further in preparation for eventual privatization. The formulation of a new Banking Law is encouraging in this regard. Fiscal policy could also help by further reducing intermediation taxes, which are high by international standards.

- **Business environment.** To improve Turkey's business environment and reduce unemployment, red tape needs to be cut further, privatization acceler-ated, and the high costs of complying with statu-tory employment protection legislation reduced.

Fulfilling this reform agenda could provide further support for Turkey's move from crisis resolution to EU accession. Turkey has already come a long way from the 2000–01 crisis. The European Council deci-sion to begin EU accession negotiations with Turkey was in many respects an endorsement and recognition of the country's progress not just in the political arena, but also in the economic sphere. The challenge now is to sustain and advance these gains. This paper has identified at least some of the economic reforms needed to fulfill Turkey's aspirations for economic convergence with the European Union. Recent eco-nomic success bodes well for the country's future, but as always there are no guarantees that those successes will be sustained. Continuing sound macroeconomic policies and advancing structural reforms are ulti-mately the only secure way to provide employment and improve the living standards of Turkey's young and growing population.

References

Alesina, Alberto, and Roberto Perotti, 1996, "Fixed Adjustments in OECD Countries: Composition and Macroeconomic Effects," IMF Working Paper 96/70 (Washington: International Monetary Fund).

Allen, Mark, Christoph Rosenberg, Christian Keller, Brad Setser, and Nouriel Roubini, 2002, "A Balance Sheet Approach to Financial Crisis," IMF Working Paper 02/210 (Washington: International Monetary Fund).

Alper, C. Emre, and Ziya Önis, 2004, "The Turkish Banking System, Financial Crises and the IMF in the Age of Capital Account Liberalization: A Political Economy Perspective," *New Perspectives on Turkey* No. 30 (Istanbul: History Foundation of Turkey).

Anand, Ritu, Ajay Chhibber, and Sweder van Wijnbergen, 1988, "External Balance, Fiscal Policy, and Growth in Turkey," World Bank Policy, Planning, and Research Working Paper 86 (Washington: World Bank).

Barro, Robert J., and Jong-Wha Lee, 2000, "International Data on Educational Attainment: Updates and Implications," CID Working Paper No. 42 (Cambridge, MA: Center for International Development at Harvard University).

Blanchard, Oliver, 2004, "Fiscal Dominance and Inflation Targeting: Lessons from Brazil," NBER Working Paper No. 10389 (Cambridge, MA: National Bureau of Economic Research).

Bohn, Henning, 1998, "The Behavior of U.S. Public Debt and Deficits," *Quarterly Journal of Economics,* Vol. 113 (August), pp. 949–63.

Bosworth, Barry, and Susan Collins, 2003, "The Empirics of Growth: An Update," Economics of Developing Countries Papers (September) (Washington: Brookings Institution).

Celasun, Merih, 1990, "Fiscal Aspects of Adjustment in the 1990s," in *The Political Economy of Turkey: Debt, Adjustment, and Sustainability,* ed. by Tosun Aricanli and Dani Rodrik (London: Macmillan).

Celasun, Oya, R. Gaston Gelos, and Allesandro Prati, 2003, "Would 'Cold Turkey' Work in Turkey?" IMF Working Paper 03/49 (Washington: International Monetary Fund).

———, 2004, "Obstacles to Disinflation: What is the Role of Fiscal Expectations?" *Economic Policy,* Vol. 19, No. 40 (October), pp. 441–81.

Cohen, Daniel, 2000, "The HIPC Initiative: True and False Promises," Organization for Economic Cooperation and Development Centre Working Paper No. 166 (Paris: OECD Development Centre).

Dutz, Mark, Melek Us, and Kamil Yilmaz, 2005, "Turkey's Foreign Direct Investment Challenges: Competition, the Rule of Law, and EU Accession," in *Turkey: Towards EU Accession,* ed. by Bernard Hoekman and Subidey Togan (Oxford: Oxford University Press for the World Bank).

Easterly, William, 2001, "The Lost Decades: Developing Countries' Stagnation in Spite of Policy Reform, 1980–1998," *Journal of Economic Growth,* Vol. 6, No. 2, pp. 135–57.

Erzan, Refik, Alpay Filiztekin, and Unal Zenginobuz, 2003, "Impact of the Customs Union with EU on Turkish Manufacturing Industry," paper presented at the ninth annual conference of the Economic Research Forum, United Arab Emirates, October 26–28.

Fatás, Antonio, and Ilian Mihov, 2003, "The Case for Restricting Fiscal Policy Discretion," *Quarterly Journal of Economics,* Vol. 118, No. 4 (November), pp.1419–47.

Favero, Carlo, 2002, "How Do European Monetary and Fiscal Authorities Behave?" Center for Economic Policy Research Discussion Paper No. 3426 (London: Centre for Economic Policy Research).

———, and Francesco Giavazzi, 2004, "Inflation Targeting and Debt: Lessons from Brazil," Center for Economic Policy Research Discussion Paper No. 4376 (London: Centre for Economic Policy Research).

Gali, Jordi, and Mark Gertler, 1999, "Inflation Dynamics: A Structural Econometric Analysis," *Journal of Monetary Economics,* Vol. 44, Issue 2, pp. 195–222.

———, and Roberto Perotti, 2003, "Fiscal Policy and Monetary Integration in Europe," *Economic Policy,* Vol. 18 No. 37 (October), pp. 535–72.

Garcia, Marcio, and Roberto Rigobon, 2004, "A Risk Management Approach to Emerging Market's Sovereign Debt Sustainability with an Application to Brazilian Data," NBER Working Paper No. 10336 (Cambridge, MA: National Bureau of Economic Research).

Giavazzi, Francesco, 2003, "Inflation Targeting and Fiscal Policy Regime: The Experience of Brazil," *Bank of England Quarterly Bulletin* (Autumn).

Goldstein, Morris, 2003, "Debt Sustainability, Brazil, and the IMF," IIE Working Paper 03-1 (Washington: Institute for International Economics).

———, and Philip Turner, 2004, *Controlling Currency Mismatches in Emerging Markets* (Washington: Institute of International Economics).

Gupta, Sanjeev, Emanuele Baldacci, Benedict J. Clements, and Erwin R. Tiongson, 2003, "What Sustains Fiscal Consolidations in Emerging Market Countries?" IMF Working Paper 02/224 (Washington: International Monetary Fund).

Heston, Alan, Robert Summers, and Bettina Aten, 2002, Penn World Table Version 6.1, Center for International Comparisons at the University of Pennsylvania (CICUP), October.

International Monetary Fund (IMF), 2003, "Public Debt in Emerging Market Economies: Is It Too High?" in *World Economic Outlook September, 2005* (Washington: International Monetary Fund).

Krueger, Anne O., 2004. "Pursuing the Achievable: Macroeconomic Stability and Sustainable Growth in Turkey," speech to the Economic Congress of Turkey, Izmir, May 5, 2004, *www.imf.org/external/np/speeches/2004/050504.htm.*

———, and Okan H. Aktan, 1992, *Swimming Against the Tide: Turkish Trade Reforms in the 1980s* (San Francisco: International Center for Economic Growth, ICS Press.

Kruger, Mark, and Miguel Messmacher, 2004, "Sovereign Debt Defaults and Financing Needs," IMF Working Paper 04/53 (Washington: International Monetary Fund).

Maddison, Angus, 2001, *The World Economy: Historical Statistics* (Paris: Organization for Economic Cooperation and Development Centre).

Manasse, Paolo, Nouriel Roubini, and Axel Schimmelpfennig, 2003, "Predicting Sovereign Debt Crisis," IMF Working Paper 03/221 (Washington: International Monetary Fund).

Mody, Ashoka, and Martin Schindler, 2004, "Argentina's Growth: A Puzzle?" (unpublished; Washington: International Monetary Fund).

Önis, Ziya, 2004, "Turgut Ozal and His Economic Legacy: Turkish Neo-Liberalism in Critical Perspective," *Middle Eastern Studies* Vol. 40, No. 4.

———, and James Riedel, 1993, *Economic Crises and Long-Term Growth in Turkey,* World Bank Comparative Macroeconomic Studies, Vol. 1 (Washington: World Bank).

Ozler, Sule, and Kamil Yilmaz, 2004, "Does Trade Liberalization Improve Productivity? Plant Level Evidence from Turkish Manufacturing Industry" (unpublished; Istanbul: Koc University).

Pattillo, Catherine, Helene Poirson, and Luca Ricci, 2004, "Through What Channels Does External Debt Affect Growth?" in *Brookings Trade Forum 2003,* ed. by Susan M. Collins and Dani Rodrik (Washington: Brookings Institution), pp. 229–77.

Political Risk Services Group, 2003, International Country Risk Guide, *www.ICRGOnline.com.*

Ramey, Garey, and Valerie A. Ramey, 1995, "Cross-Country Evidence on the Link Between Volatility and Growth," *American Economic Review,* Vol. 85, No. 5, pp. 1138–51.

Reinhart, Carmen, Kenneth Rogoff, and Miguel Savastano, 2003, "Debt Intolerance," NBER Working Paper No. 9908 (Cambridge, MA: National Bureau of Economic Research).

Rodrik, Dani, 1999, "Where Did All the Growth Go? External Shocks, Social Conflict, and Growth Collapses," *Journal of Economic Growth,* Vol. 4, No. 4, pp. 385–412.

Sancak, Cemile, 2002, "Financial Liberalization and Real Investment: Evidence from Turkish Firms," IMF Working Paper 02/100 (Washington: International Monetary Fund).

Sargent, Thomas, and Neil Wallace, 1981, "Some Unpleasant Monetarist Arithmetic," *Federal Reserve Bank of Minneapolis Quarterly Review,* Vol. 5, No. 3 (Fall).

Shiller, Robert, 1997, "Public Resistance to Indexation: A Puzzle," *Brookings Papers on Economic Activity,* No. 1, pp. 159–228.

Talvi, Ernesto, and Carlos Végh, 2000, "Tax Base Variability and Procyclical Fiscal Policy," NBER Working Paper No. 7499 (Cambridge, MA: National Bureau for Economic Research).

Tornell, Aaron, and Philip Lane, 1999, "The Voracity Effect," *American Economic Review,* Vol. 89, No. 1 (March), pp. 22–46.

———, Frank Westermann, and Lorenza Martinez, 2004, "The Positive Link Between Financial Liberalization, Growth and Crises," NBER Working Paper No. 10293 (Cambridge, MA: National Bureau of Economic Research).

Wacziarg, Romain, and Karen Horn Welch, 2003, "Trade Liberalization and Growth: New Evidence" (unpublished; Stanford, CA: Stanford University).

Waterbury, John, 1992, "Export-Led Growth and the Center-Right Coalition in Turkey." *Comparative Politics,* Vol. 24, No. 2, pp. 127–45.

Woodford, Michael, 2001, "Fiscal Requirements For Price Stability," *Journal of Money, Credit, and Banking,* Vol. 33, No. 3.

World Bank, 2001, "Turkey - Public Expenditure and Institutional Review: Reforming Budgetary Institutions for Effective Government," World Bank Economic Report, Vol. 1, No. 22530-TU (Washington: World Bank).

Recent Occasional Papers of the International Monetary Fund

242. Turkey at the Crossroads: From Crisis Resolution to EU Accession, by a team led by Reza Moghadam. 2005.

241. The Design of IMF-Supported Programs, by Atish Ghosh, Charis Christofides, Jun Kim, Laura Papi, Uma Ramakrishnan, Alun Thomas, and Juan Zalduendo. 2005.

240. Debt-Related Vulnerabilities and Financial Crises: An Application of the Balance Sheet Approach to Emerging Market Countries, by Christoph Rosenberg, Ioannis Halikias, Brett House, Christian Keller, Jens Nystedt, Alexander Pitt, and Brad Setser. 2005.

239. GEM: A New International Macroeconomic Model, by Tamim Bayoumi, with assistance from Douglas Laxton, Hamid Faruqee, Benjamin Hunt, Philippe Karam, Jaewoo Lee, Alessandro Rebucci, and Ivan Tchakarov. 2004.

238. Stabilization and Reforms in Latin America: A Macroeconomic Perspective on the Experience Since the Early 1990s, by Anoop Singh, Agnès Belaisch, Charles Collyns, Paula De Masi, Reva Krieger, Guy Meredith, and Robert Rennhack. 2005.

237. Sovereign Debt Structure for Crisis Prevention, by Eduardo Borensztein, Marcos Chamon, Olivier Jeanne, Paolo Mauro, and Jeromin Zettelmeyer. 2004.

236. Lessons from the Crisis in Argentina, by Christina Daseking, Atish R. Ghosh, Alun Thomas, and Timothy Lane. 2004.

235. A New Look at Exchange Rate Volatility and Trade Flows, by Peter B. Clark, Natalia Tamirisa, and Shang-Jin Wei, with Azim Sadikov and Li Zeng. 2004.

234. Adopting the Euro in Central Europe: Challenges of the Next Step in European Integration, by Susan M. Schadler, Paulo F. Drummond, Louis Kuijs, Zuzana Murgasova, and Rachel N. van Elkan. 2004.

233. Germany's Three-Pillar Banking System: Cross-Country Perspectives in Europe, by Allan Brunner, Jörg Decressin, Daniel Hardy, and Beata Kudela. 2004.

232. China's Growth and Integration into the World Economy: Prospects and Challenges, edited by Eswar Prasad. 2004.

231. Chile: Policies and Institutions Underpinning Stability and Growth, by Eliot Kalter, Steven Phillips, Marco A. Espinosa-Vega, Rodolfo Luzio, Mauricio Villafuerte, and Manmohan Singh. 2004.

230. Financial Stability in Dollarized Countries, by Anne-Marie Gulde, David Hoelscher, Alain Ize, David Marston, and Gianni De Nicoló. 2004.

229. Evolution and Performance of Exchange Rate Regimes, by Kenneth S. Rogoff, Aasim M. Husain, Ashoka Mody, Robin Brooks, and Nienke Oomes. 2004.

228. Capital Markets and Financial Intermediation in The Baltics, by Alfred Schipke, Christian Beddies, Susan M. George, and Niamh Sheridan. 2004.

227. U.S. Fiscal Policies and Priorities for Long-Run Sustainability, edited by Martin Mühleisen and Christopher Towe. 2004.

226. Hong Kong SAR: Meeting the Challenges of Integration with the Mainland, edited by Eswar Prasad, with contributions from Jorge Chan-Lau, Dora Iakova, William Lee, Hong Liang, Ida Liu, Papa N'Diaye, and Tao Wang. 2004.

225. Rules-Based Fiscal Policy in France, Germany, Italy, and Spain, by Teresa Dában, Enrica Detragiache, Gabriel di Bella, Gian Maria Milesi-Ferretti, and Steven Symansky. 2003.

224. Managing Systemic Banking Crises, by a staff team led by David S. Hoelscher and Marc Quintyn. 2003.

223. Monetary Union Among Member Countries of the Gulf Cooperation Council, by a staff team led by Ugo Fasano. 2003.

222. Informal Funds Transfer Systems: An Analysis of the Informal Hawala System, by Mohammed El Qorchi, Samuel Munzele Maimbo, and John F. Wilson. 2003.

221. Deflation: Determinants, Risks, and Policy Options, by Manmohan S. Kumar. 2003.

220. Effects of Financial Globalization on Developing Countries: Some Empirical Evidence, by Eswar S. Prasad, Kenneth Rogoff, Shang-Jin Wei, and Ayhan Kose. 2003.

219. Economic Policy in a Highly Dollarized Economy: The Case of Cambodia, by Mario de Zamaroczy and Sopanha Sa. 2003.

218. Fiscal Vulnerability and Financial Crises in Emerging Market Economies, by Richard Hemming, Michael Kell, and Axel Schimmelpfennig. 2003.

217. Managing Financial Crises: Recent Experience and Lessons for Latin America, edited by Charles Collyns and G. Russell Kincaid. 2003.

216. Is the PRGF Living Up to Expectations?—An Assessment of Program Design, by Sanjeev Gupta, Mark Plant, Benedict Clements, Thomas Dorsey, Emanuele Baldacci, Gabriela Inchauste, Shamsuddin Tareq, and Nita Thacker. 2002.

215. Improving Large Taxpayers' Compliance: A Review of Country Experience, by Katherine Baer. 2002.

214. Advanced Country Experiences with Capital Account Liberalization, by Age Bakker and Bryan Chapple. 2002.

213. The Baltic Countries: Medium-Term Fiscal Issues Related to EU and NATO Accession, by Johannes Mueller, Christian Beddies, Robert Burgess, Vitali Kramarenko, and Joannes Mongardini. 2002.

212. Financial Soundness Indicators: Analytical Aspects and Country Practices, by V. Sundararajan, Charles Enoch, Armida San José, Paul Hilbers, Russell Krueger, Marina Moretti, and Graham Slack. 2002.

211. Capital Account Liberalization and Financial Sector Stability, by a staff team led by Shogo Ishii and Karl Habermeier. 2002.

210. IMF-Supported Programs in Capital Account Crises, by Atish Ghosh, Timothy Lane, Marianne Schulze-Ghattas, Aleš Bulíř, Javier Hamann, and Alex Mourmouras. 2002.

209. Methodology for Current Account and Exchange Rate Assessments, by Peter Isard, Hamid Faruqee, G. Russell Kincaid, and Martin Fetherston. 2001.

208. Yemen in the 1990s: From Unification to Economic Reform, by Klaus Enders, Sherwyn Williams, Nada Choueiri, Yuri Sobolev, and Jan Walliser. 2001.

207. Malaysia: From Crisis to Recovery, by Kanitta Meesook, Il Houng Lee, Olin Liu, Yougesh Khatri, Natalia Tamirisa, Michael Moore, and Mark H. Krysl. 2001.

206. The Dominican Republic: Stabilization, Structural Reform, and Economic Growth, by a staff team led by Philip Young comprising Alessandro Giustiniani, Werner C. Keller, and Randa E. Sab and others. 2001.

205. Stabilization and Savings Funds for Nonrenewable Resources, by Jeffrey Davis, Rolando Ossowski, James Daniel, and Steven Barnett. 2001.

204. Monetary Union in West Africa (ECOWAS): Is It Desirable and How Could It Be Achieved? by Paul Masson and Catherine Pattillo. 2001.

203. Modern Banking and OTC Derivatives Markets: The Transformation of Global Finance and Its Implications for Systemic Risk, by Garry J. Schinasi, R. Sean Craig, Burkhard Drees, and Charles Kramer. 2000.

202. Adopting Inflation Targeting: Practical Issues for Emerging Market Countries, by Andrea Schaechter, Mark R. Stone, and Mark Zelmer. 2000.

201. Developments and Challenges in the Caribbean Region, by Samuel Itam, Simon Cueva, Erik Lundback, Janet Stotsky, and Stephen Tokarick. 2000.

200. Pension Reform in the Baltics: Issues and Prospects, by Jerald Schiff, Niko Hobdari, Axel Schimmelpfennig, and Roman Zytek. 2000.

199. Ghana: Economic Development in a Democratic Environment, by Sérgio Pereira Leite, Anthony Pellechio, Luisa Zanforlin, Girma Begashaw, Stefania Fabrizio, and Joachim Harnack. 2000.

198. Setting Up Treasuries in the Baltics, Russia, and Other Countries of the Former Soviet Union: An Assessment of IMF Technical Assistance, by Barry H. Potter and Jack Diamond. 2000.

197. Deposit Insurance: Actual and Good Practices, by Gillian G.H. Garcia. 2000.

196. Trade and Trade Policies in Eastern and Southern Africa, by a staff team led by Arvind Subramanian, with Enrique Gelbard, Richard Harmsen, Katrin Elborgh-Woytek, and Piroska Nagy. 2000.

Note: For information on the titles and availability of Occasional Papers not listed, please consult the IMF's *Publications Catalog* or contact IMF Publication Services.